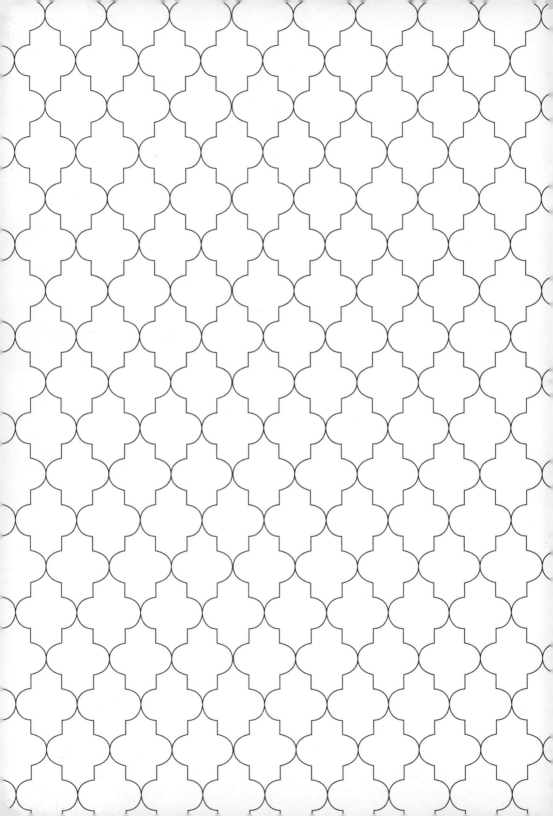

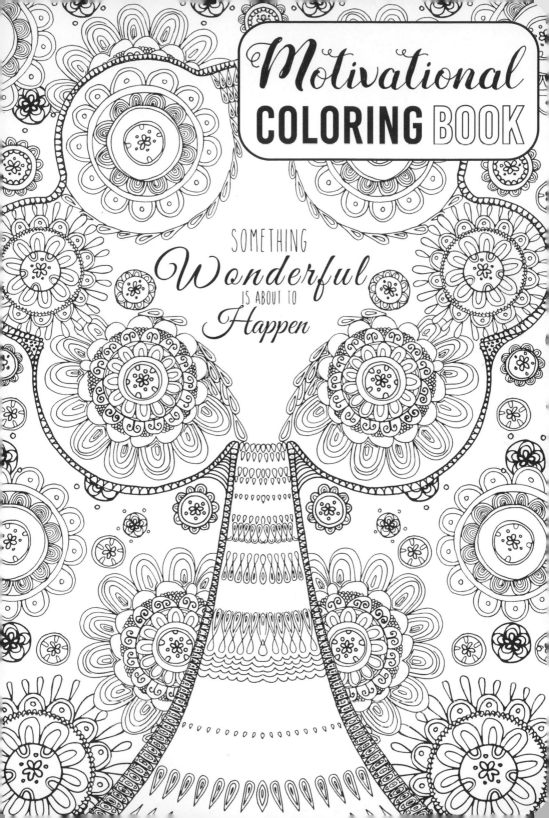

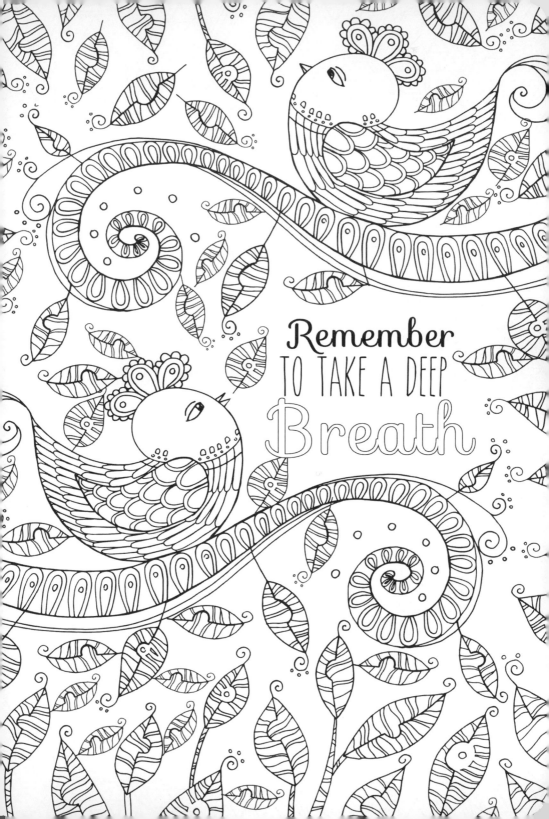

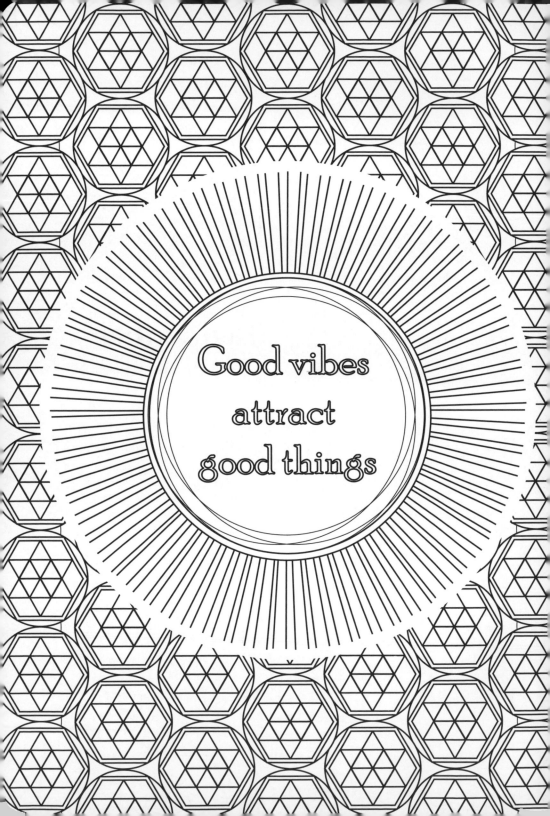

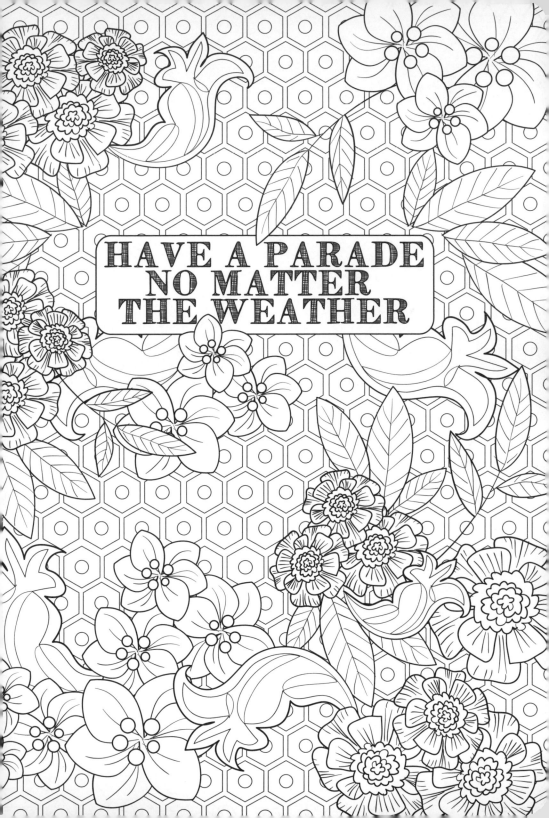

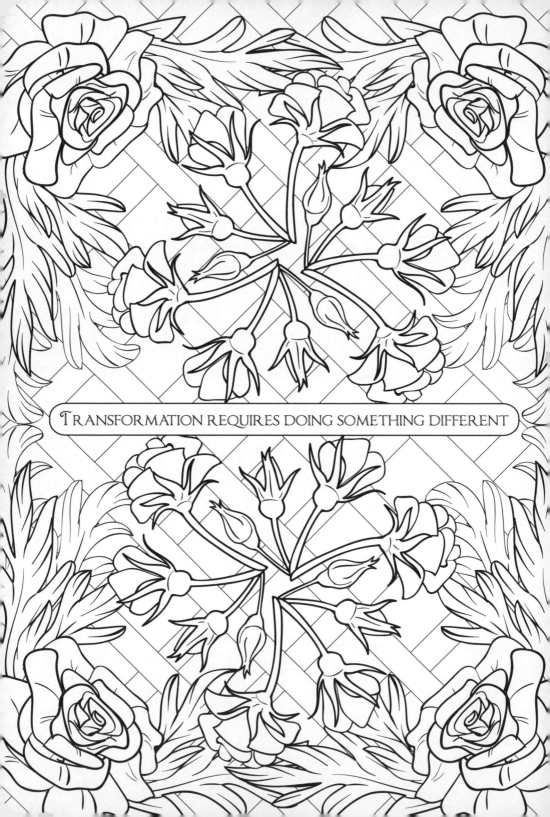

Transformation requires doing something different

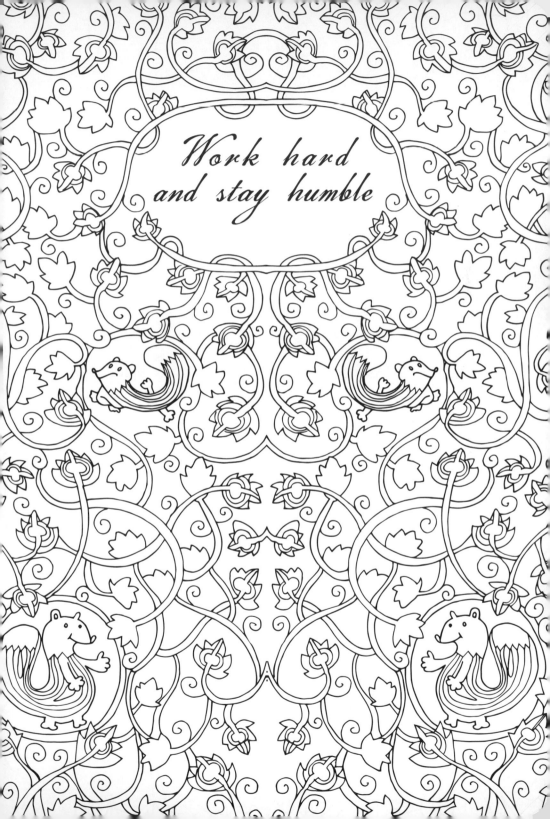

Work hard
and stay humble

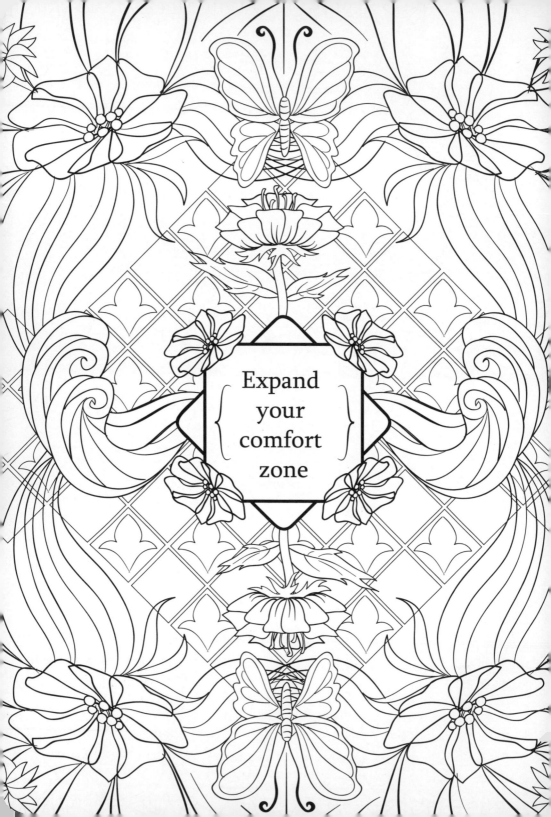

{ Expand
your
comfort
zone }

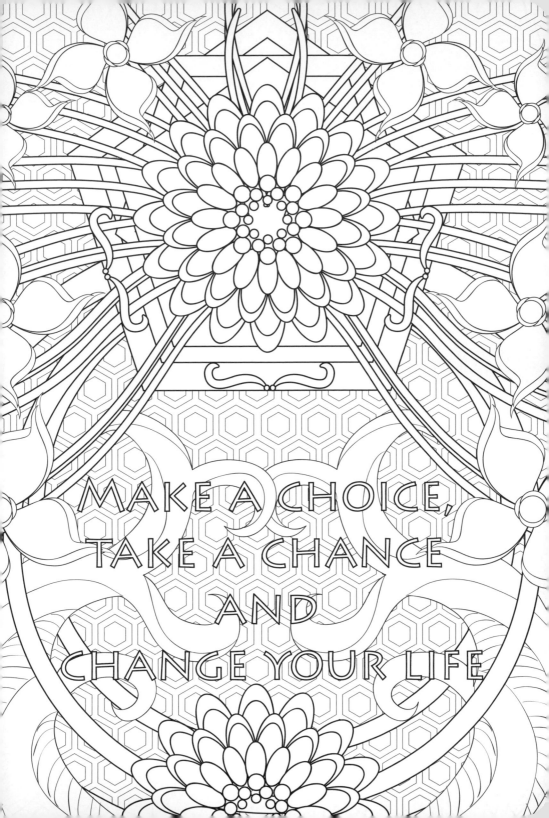

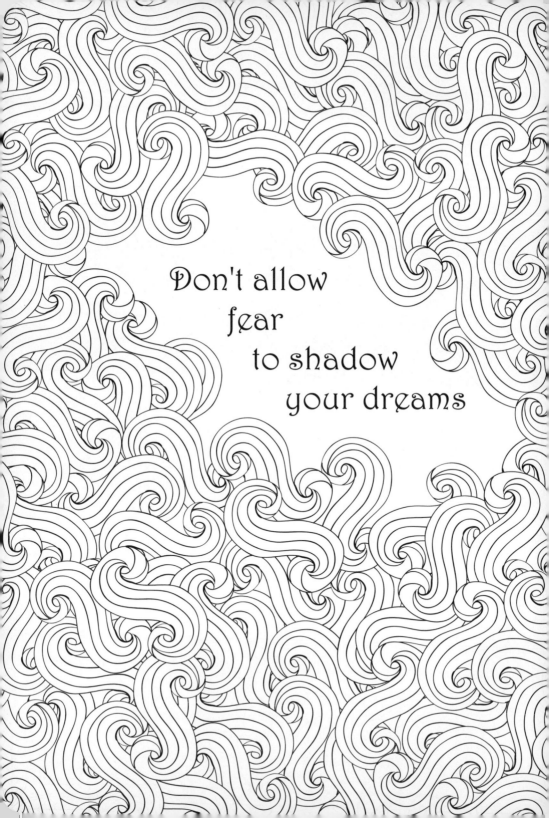

Don't allow
fear
to shadow
your dreams

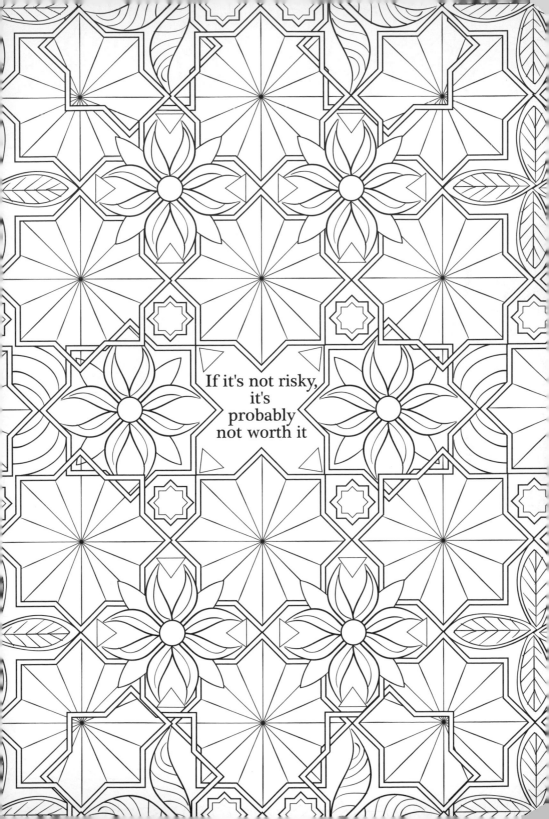

If it's not risky,
it's
probably
not worth it

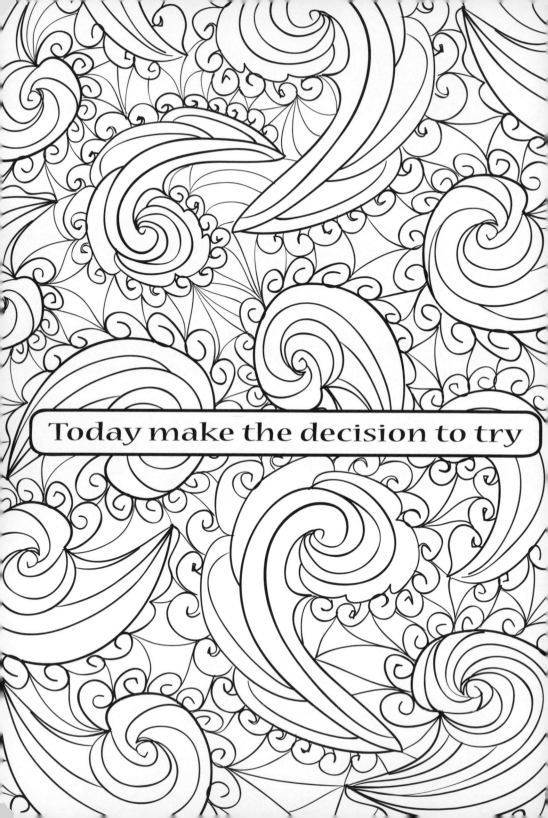

Today make the decision to try

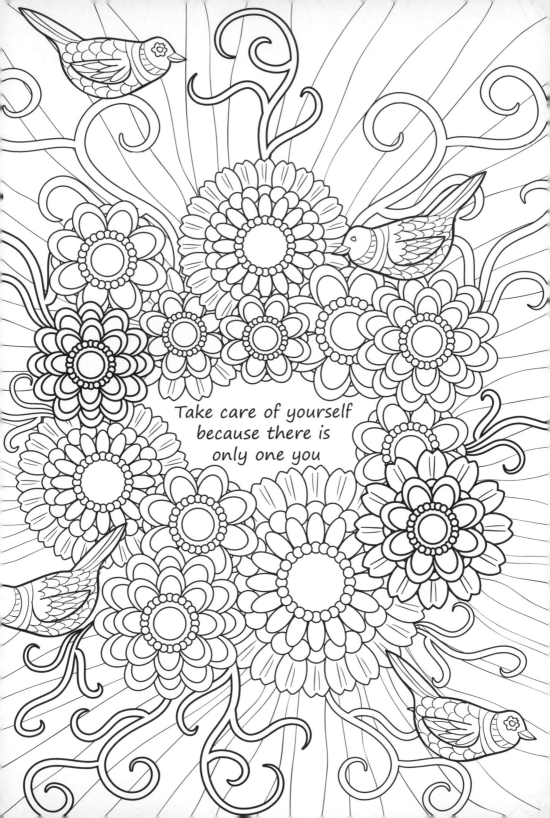

Take care of yourself
because there is
only one you

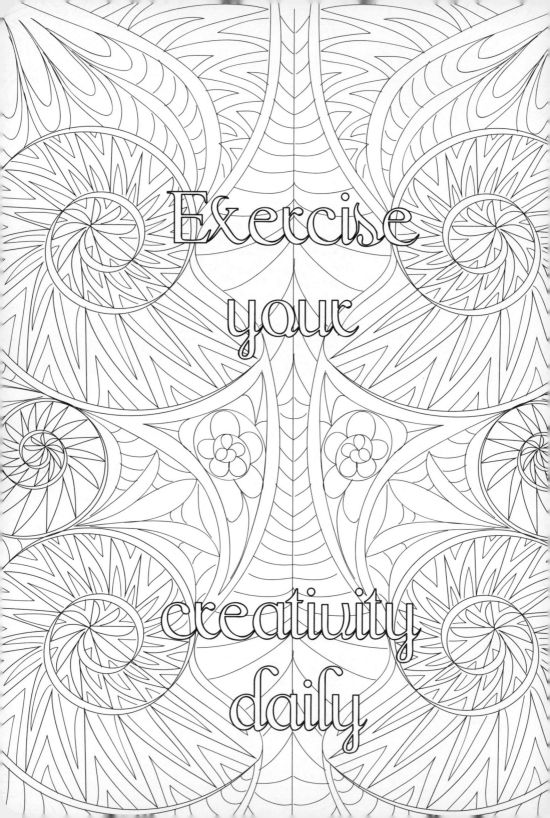

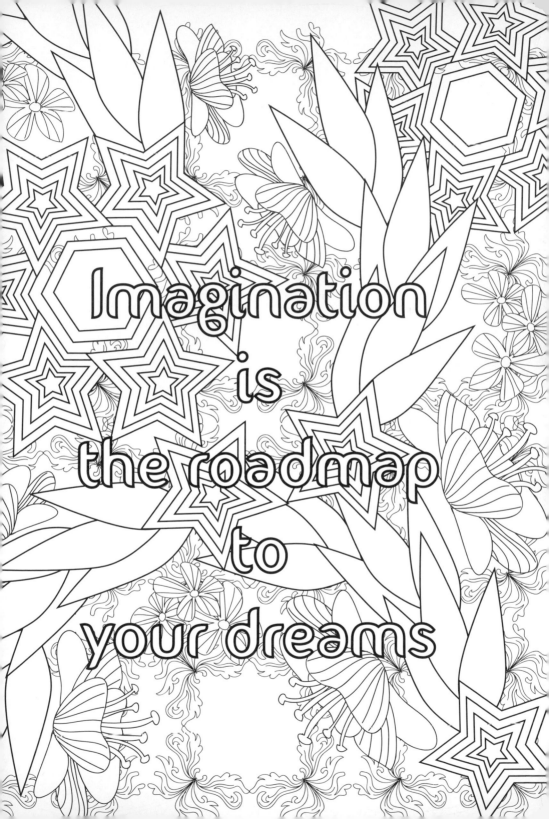

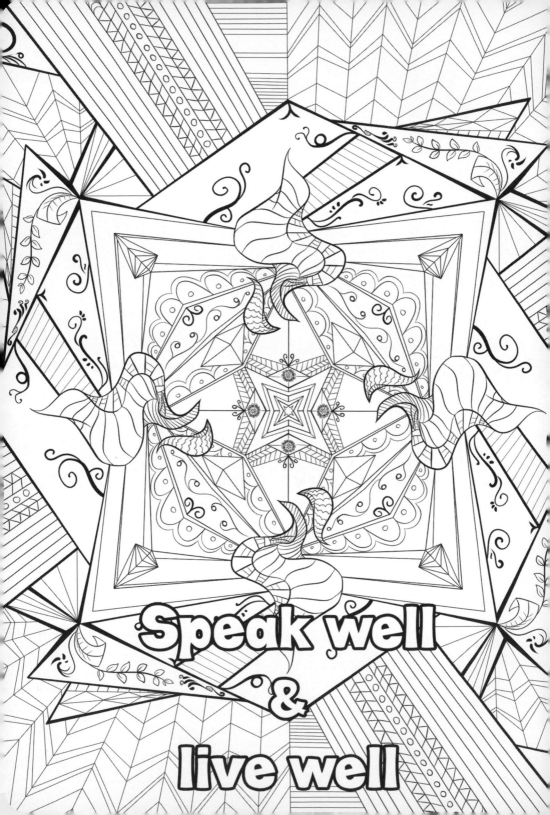

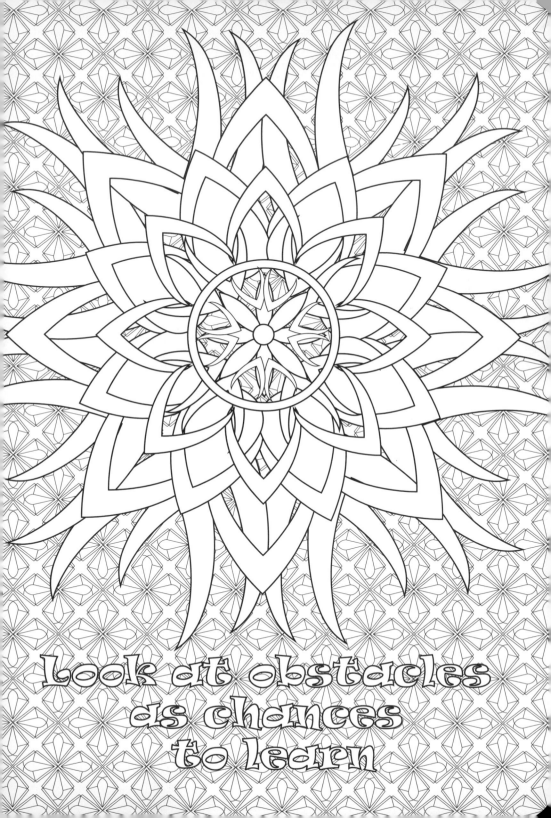

Look at obstacles
as chances
to learn

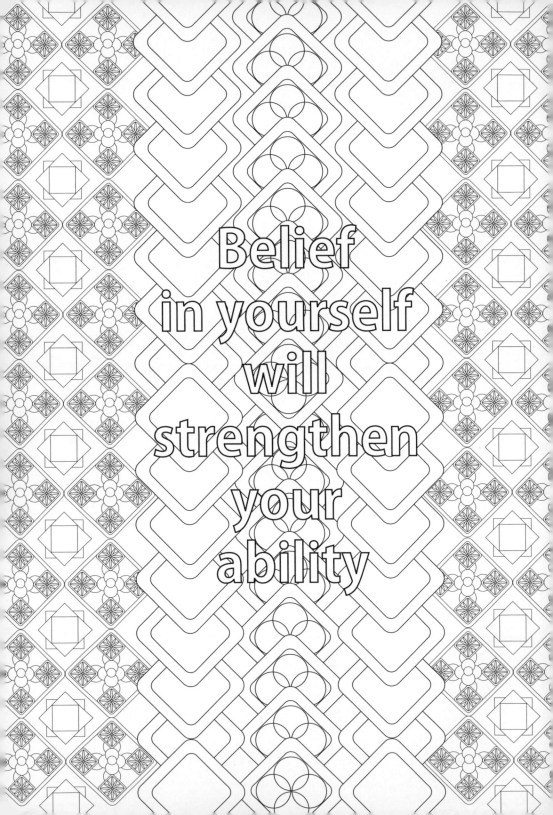

Belief
in yourself
will
strengthen
your
ability

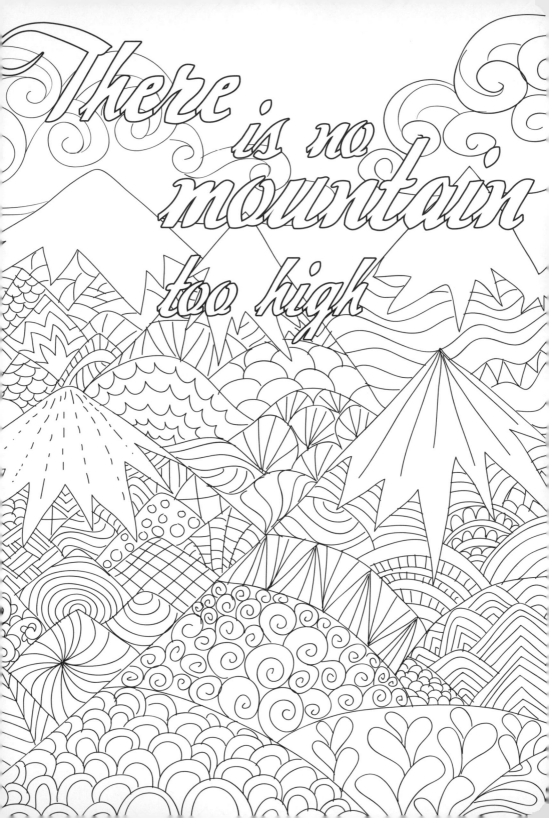

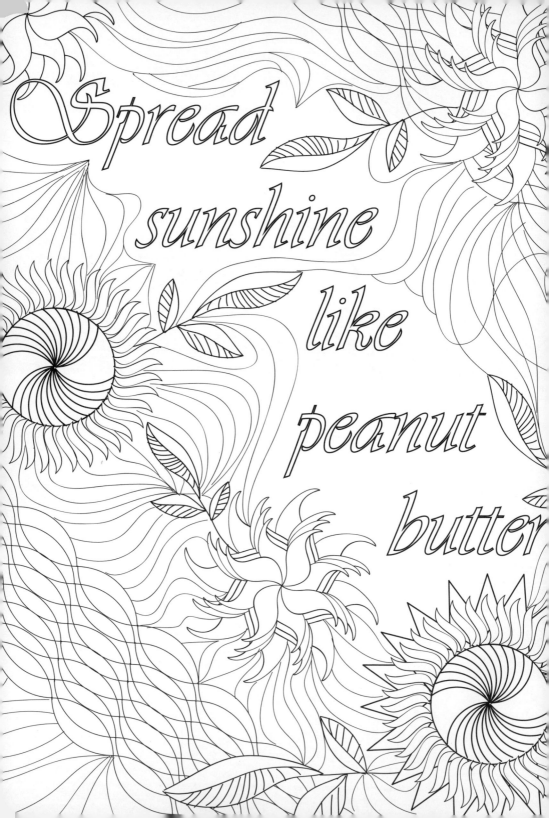

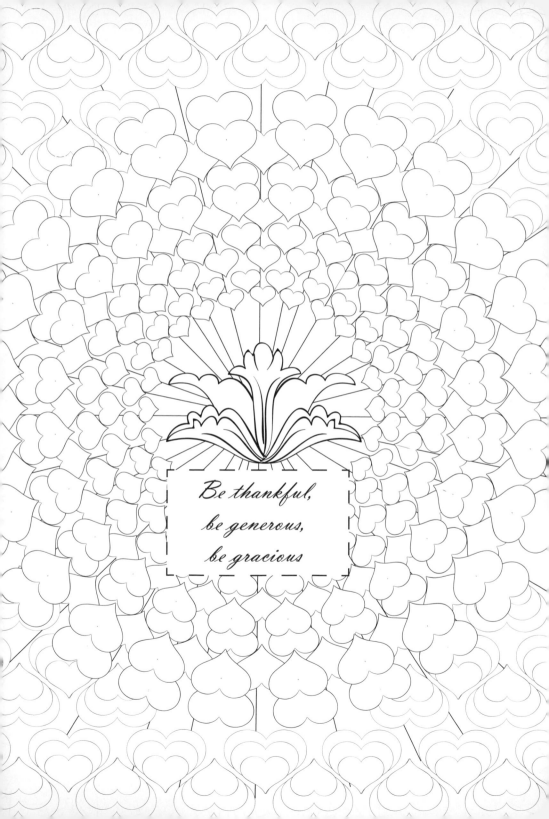

Be thankful,
be generous,
be gracious

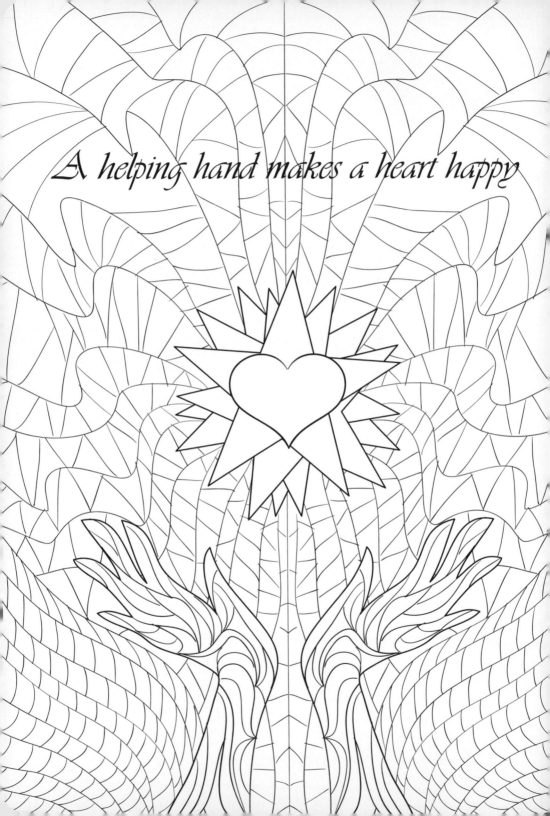

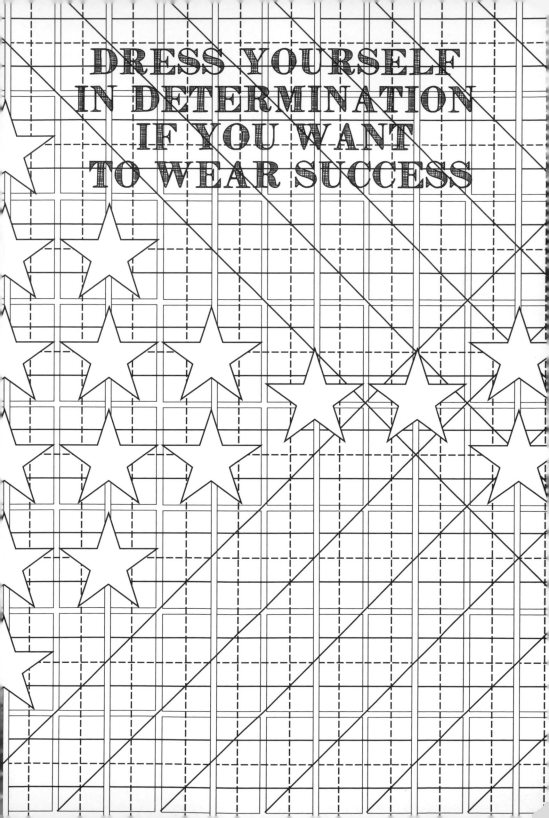

DRESS YOURSELF
IN DETERMINATION
IF YOU WANT
TO WEAR SUCCESS

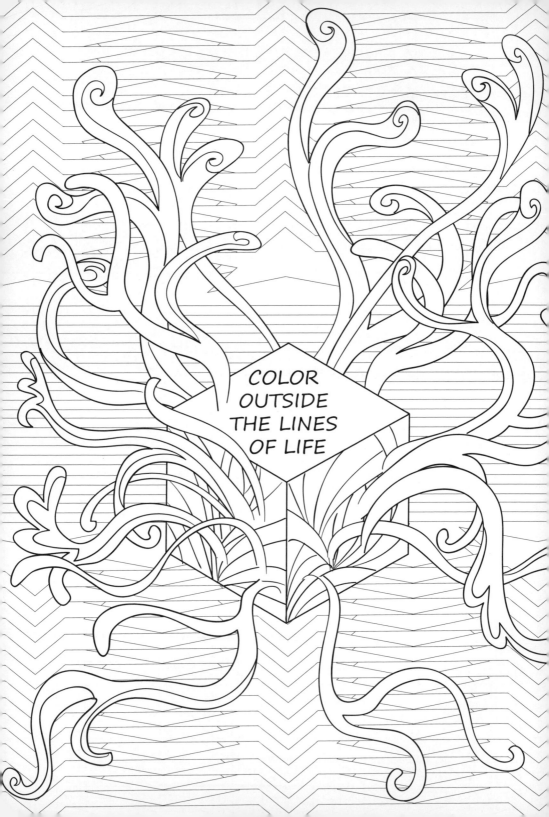

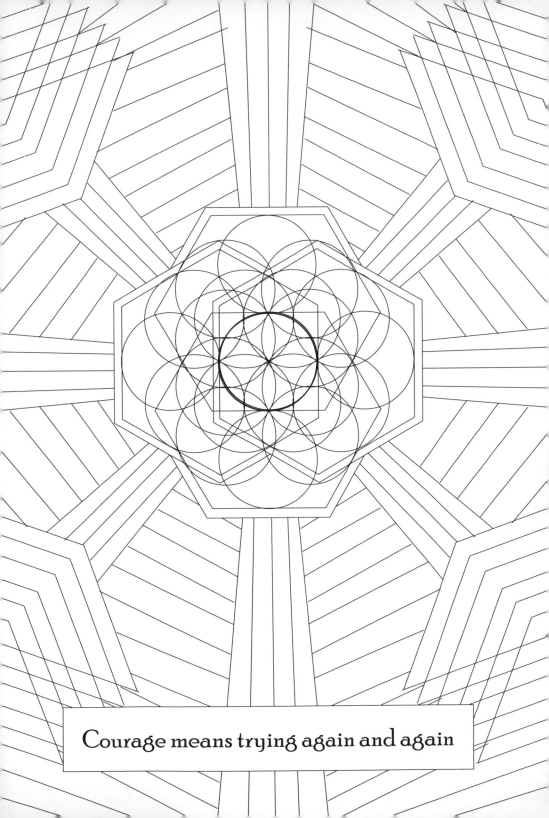

Courage means trying again and again

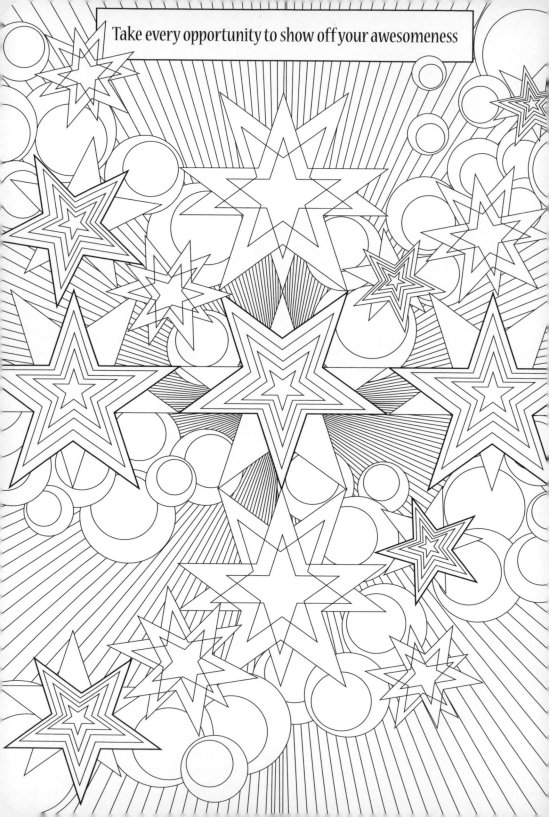

Take every opportunity to show off your awesomeness

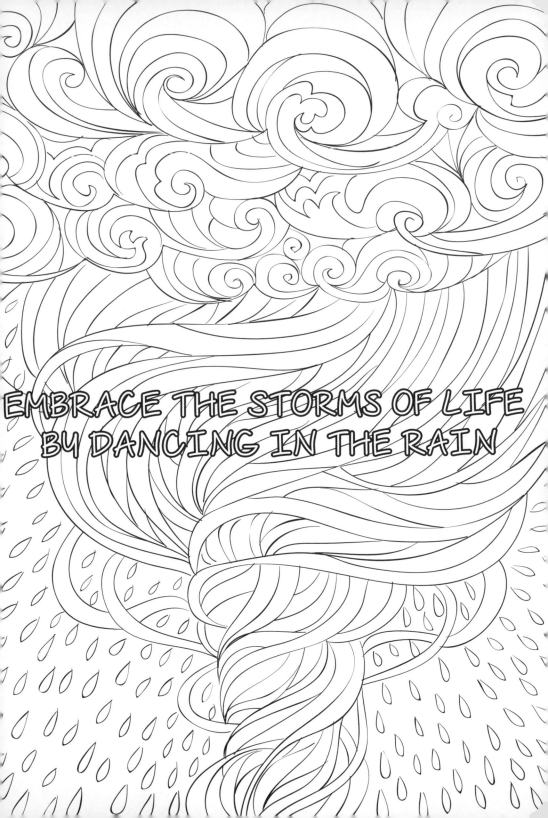

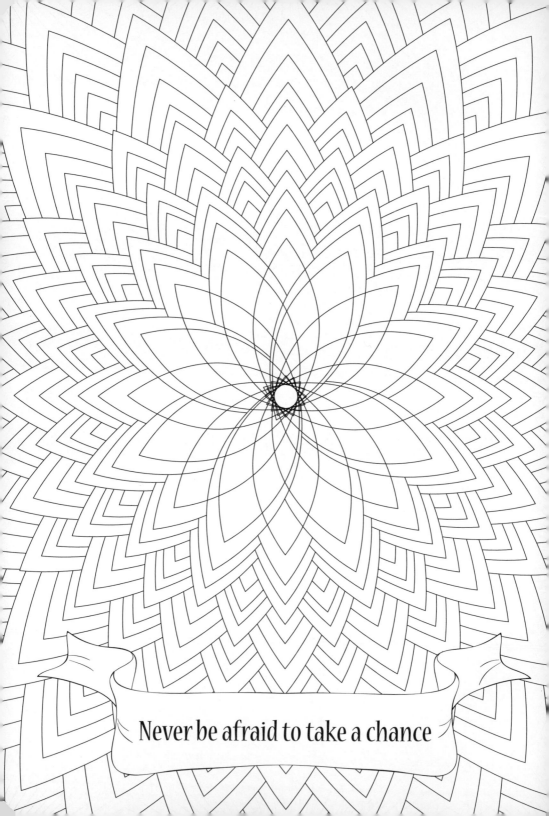

Never be afraid to take a chance

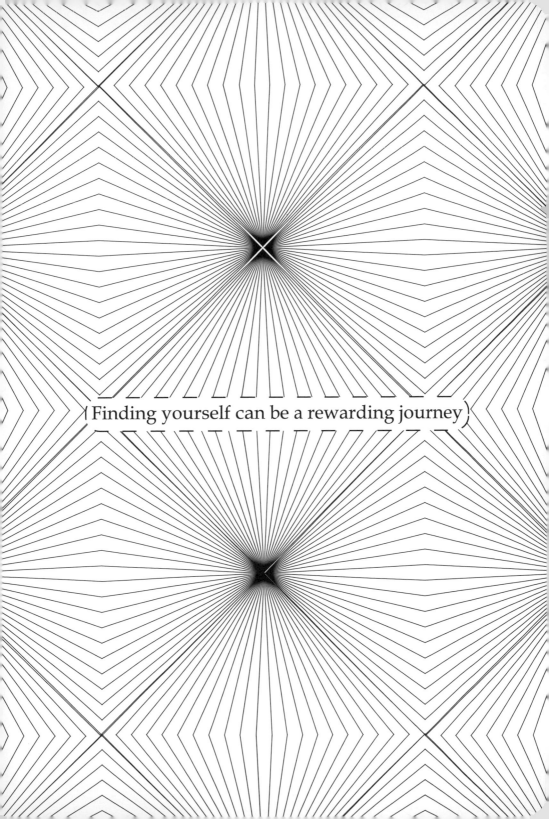

{ Finding yourself can be a rewarding journey }

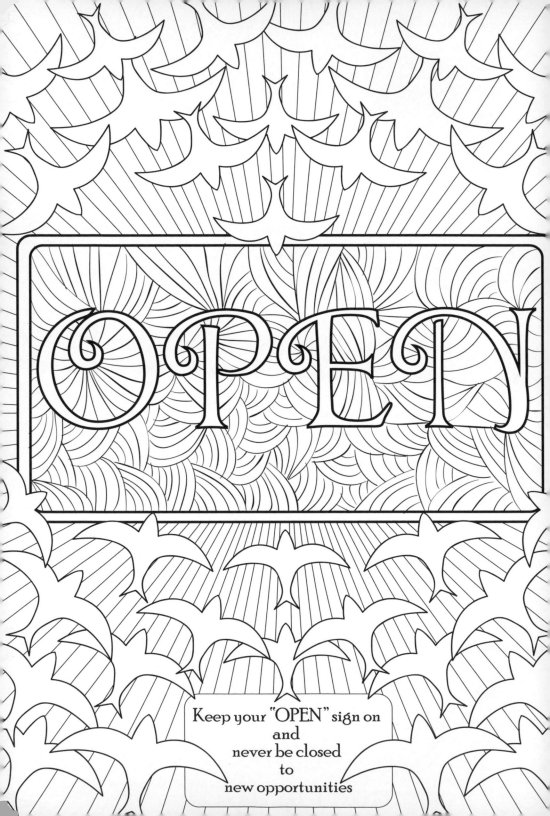

OPEN

Keep your "OPEN" sign on
and
never be closed
to
new opportunities

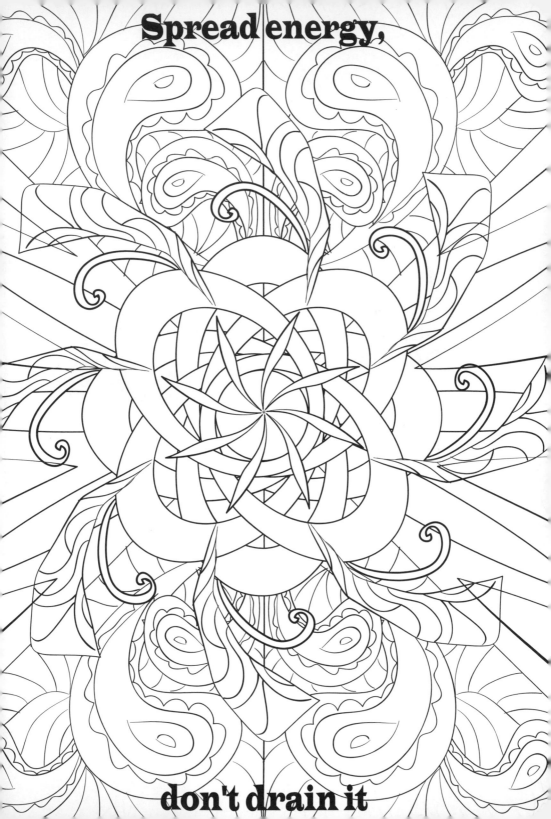

Spread energy,

don't drain it

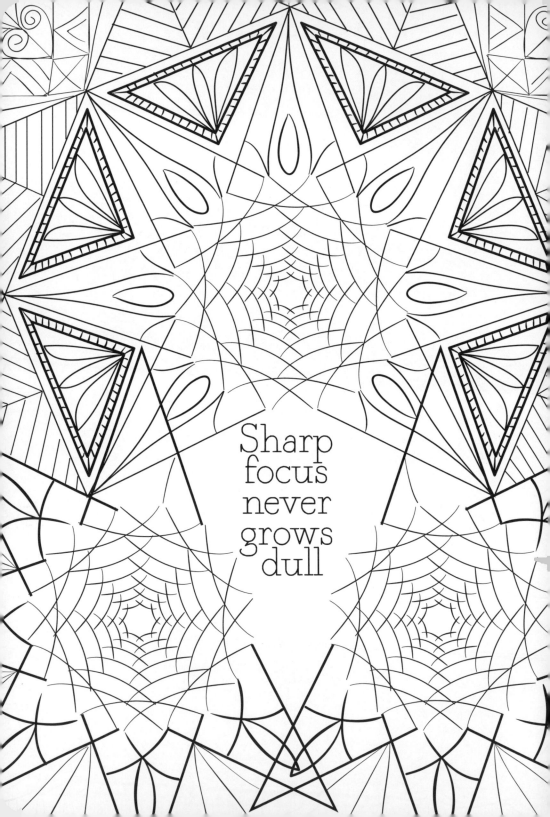

Sharp
focus
never
grows
dull

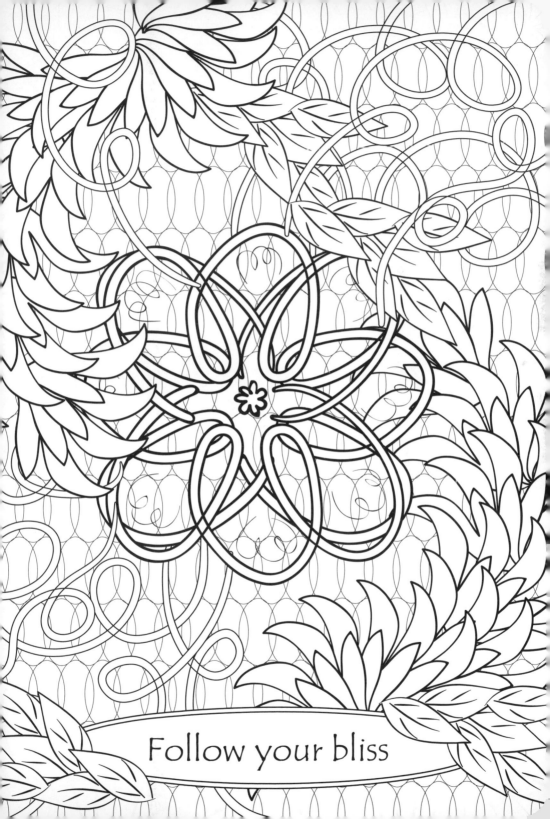

Follow your bliss

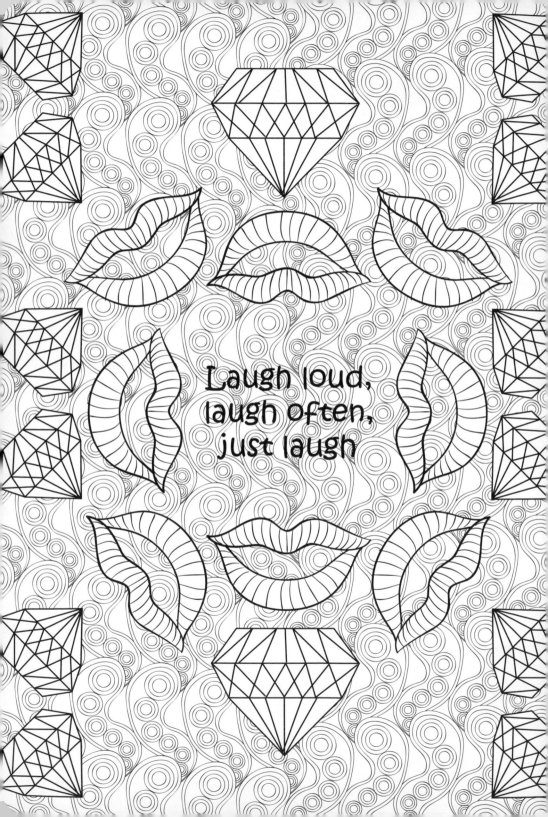

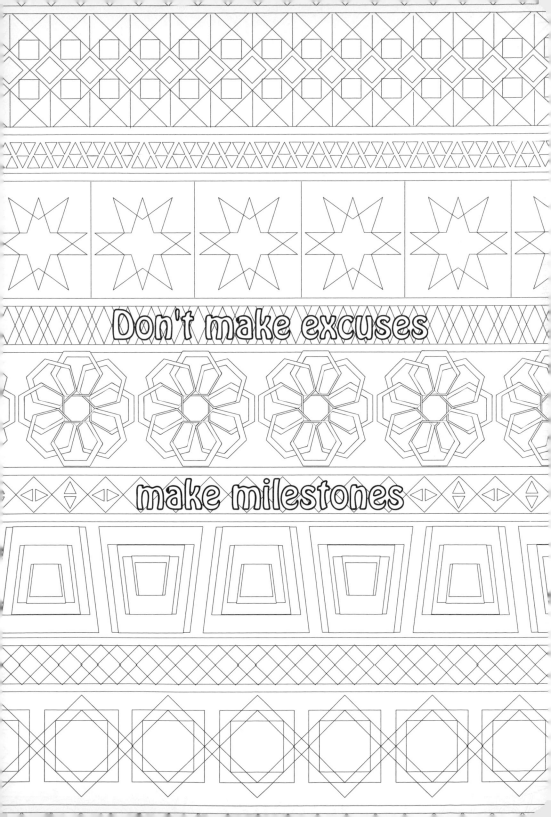

Don't make excuses

make milestones

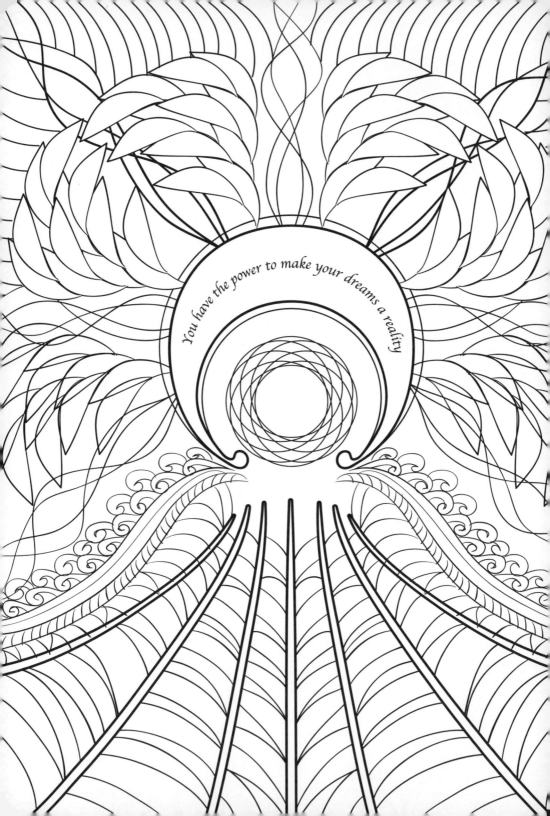

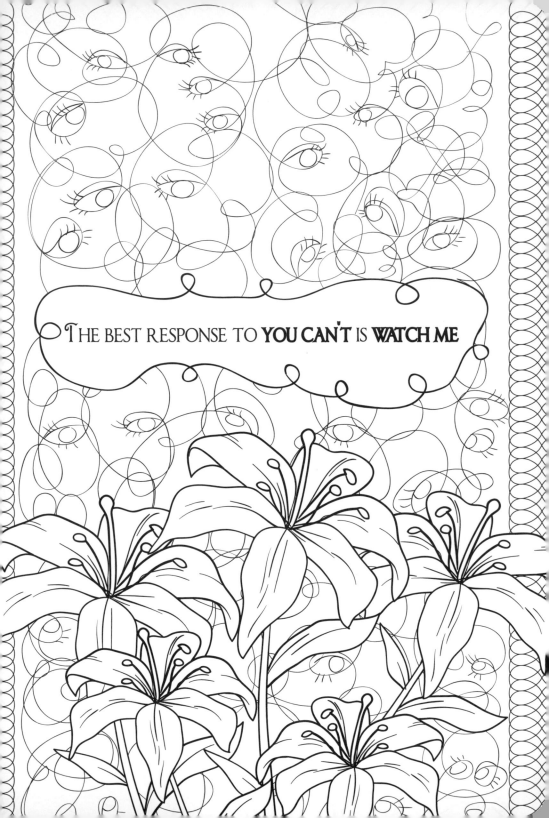

THE BEST RESPONSE TO **YOU CAN'T** IS **WATCH ME**

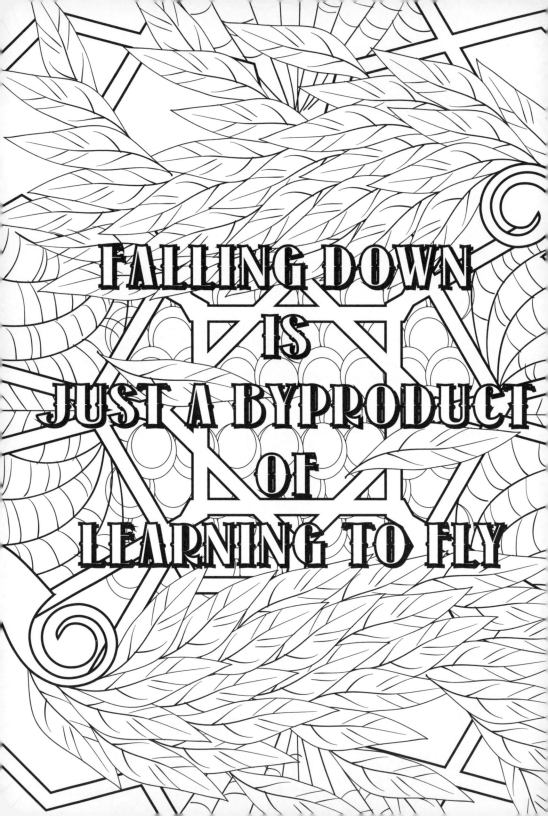

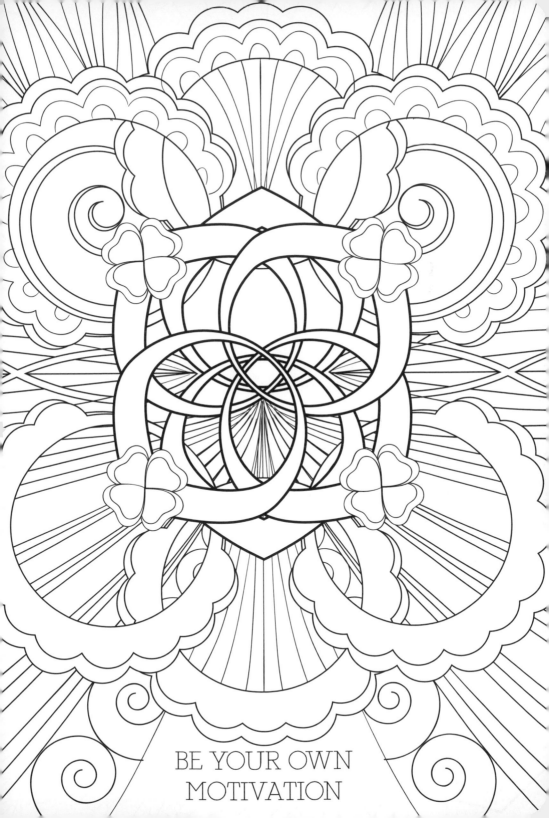

BE YOUR OWN
MOTIVATION

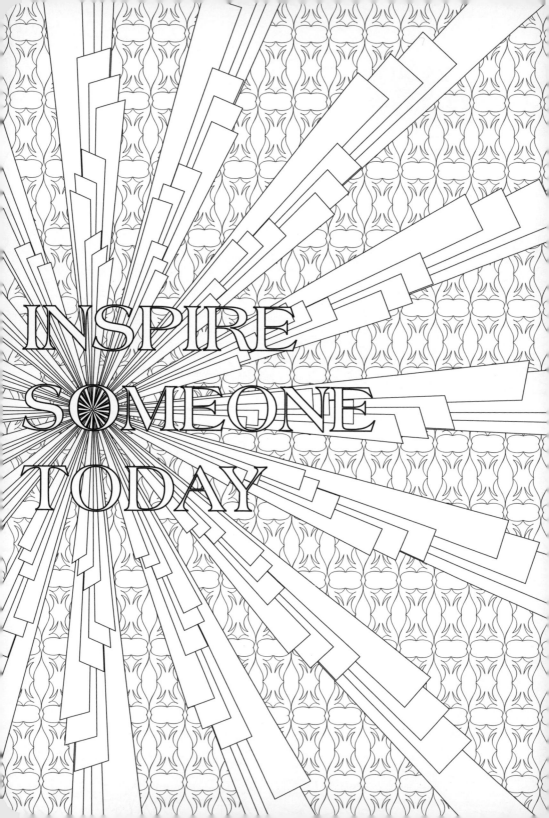

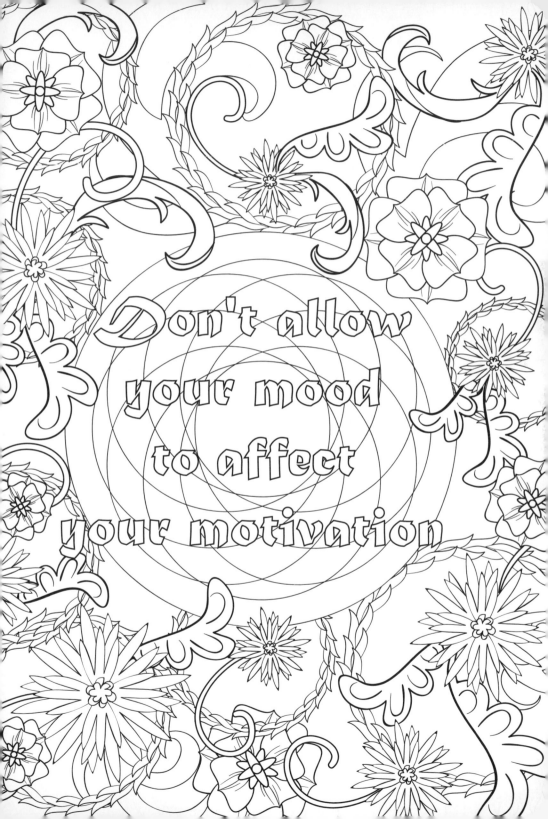

Don't allow your mood to affect your motivation

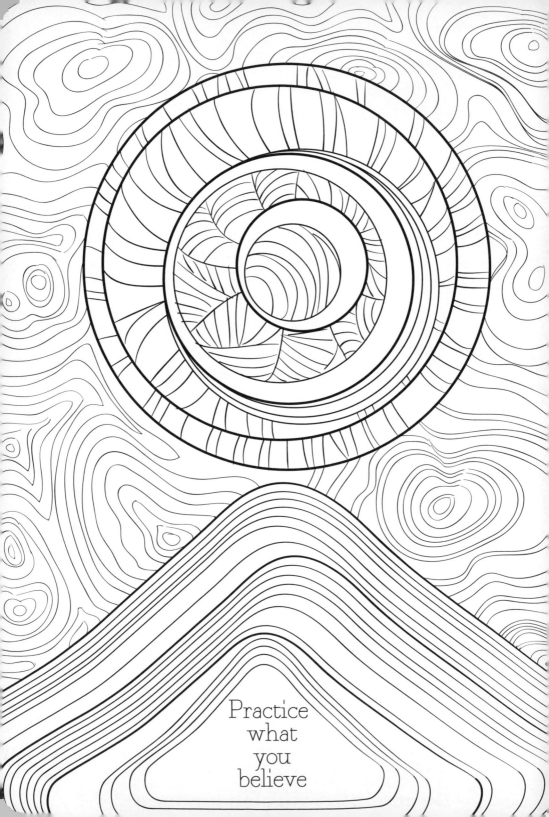

Practice
what
you
believe

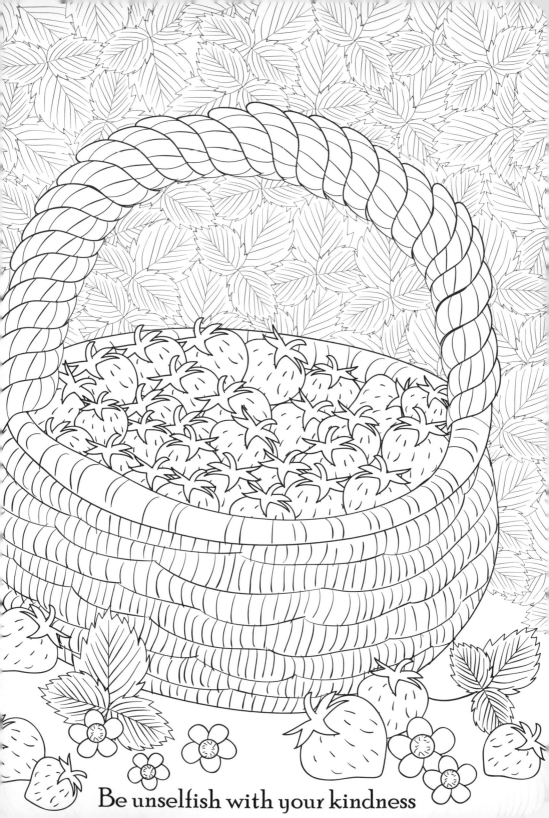

Be unselfish with your kindness

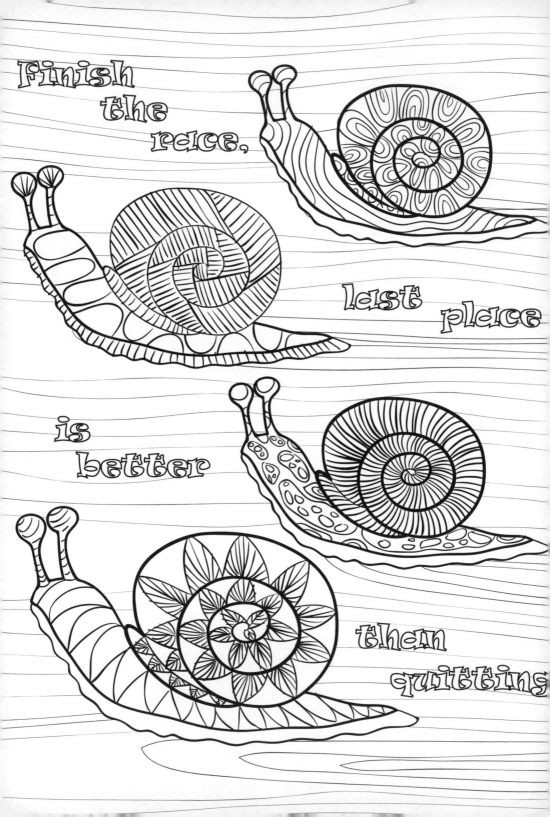

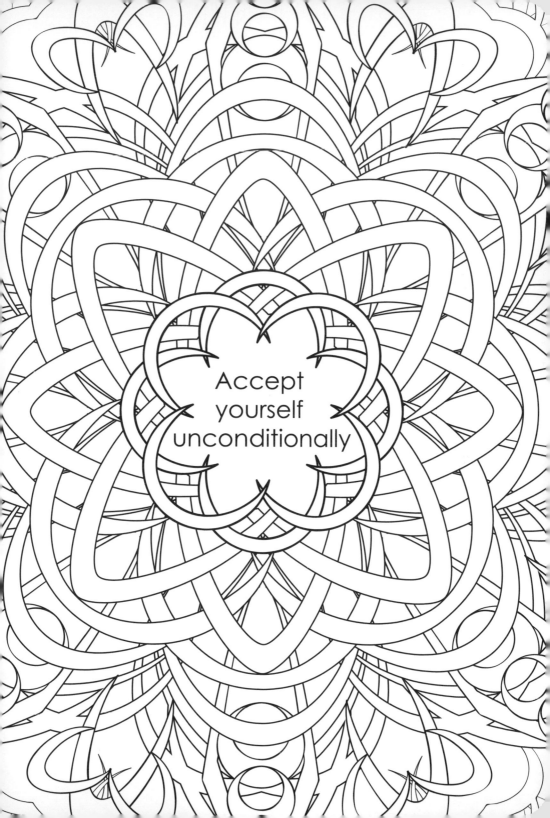

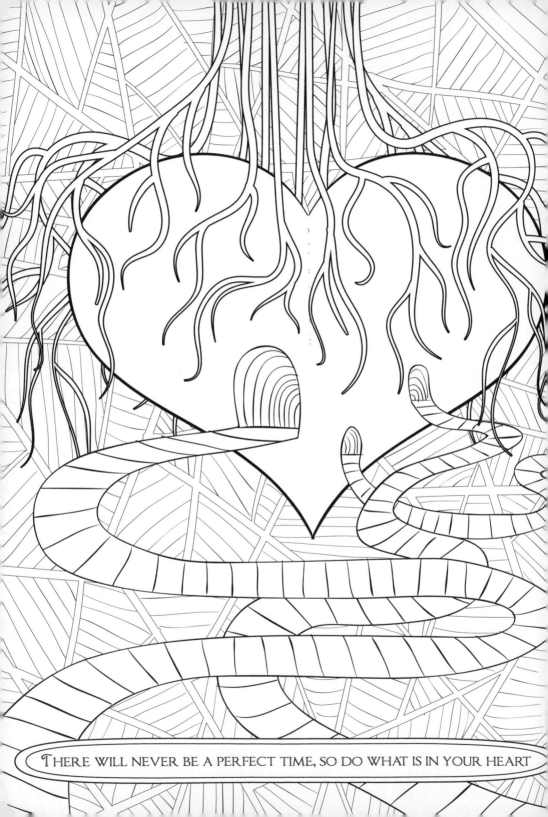

THERE WILL NEVER BE A PERFECT TIME, SO DO WHAT IS IN YOUR HEART

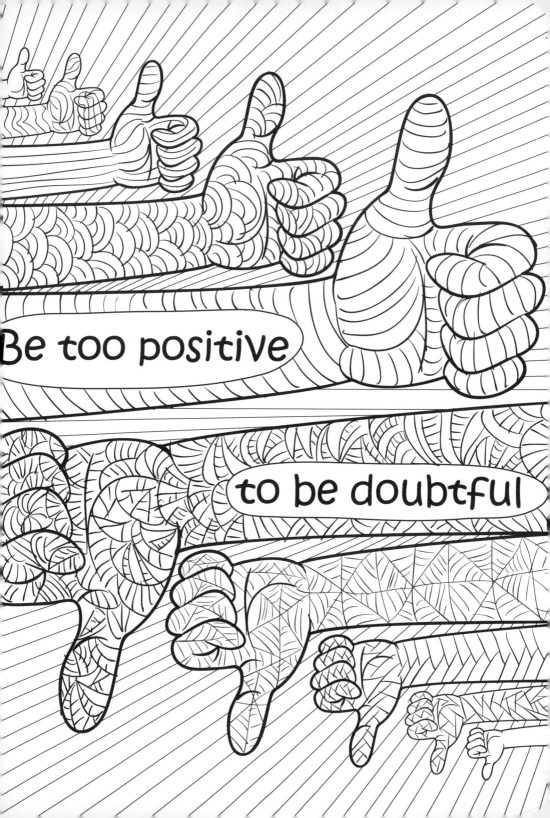

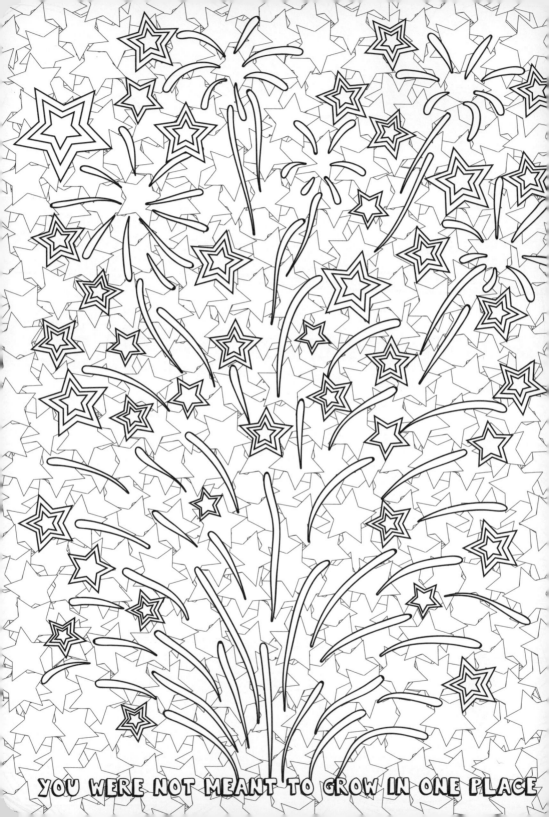

YOU WERE NOT MEANT TO GROW IN ONE PLACE

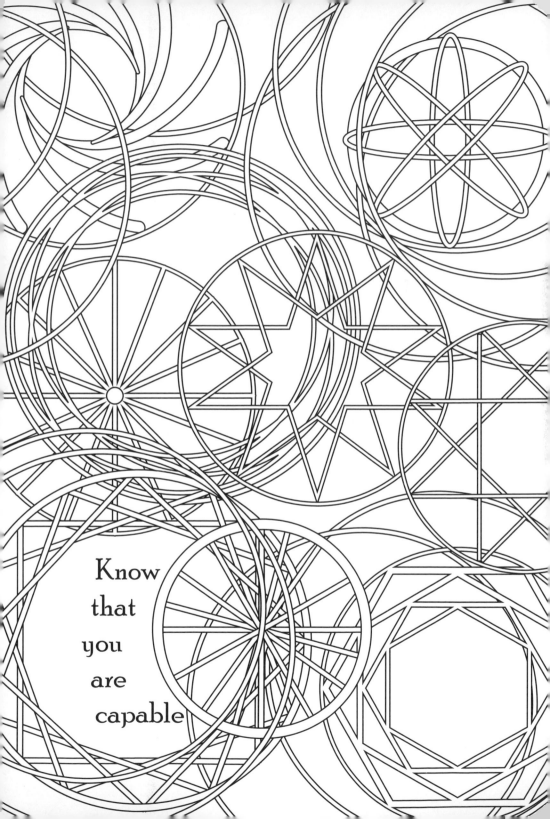

Know
that
you
are
capable

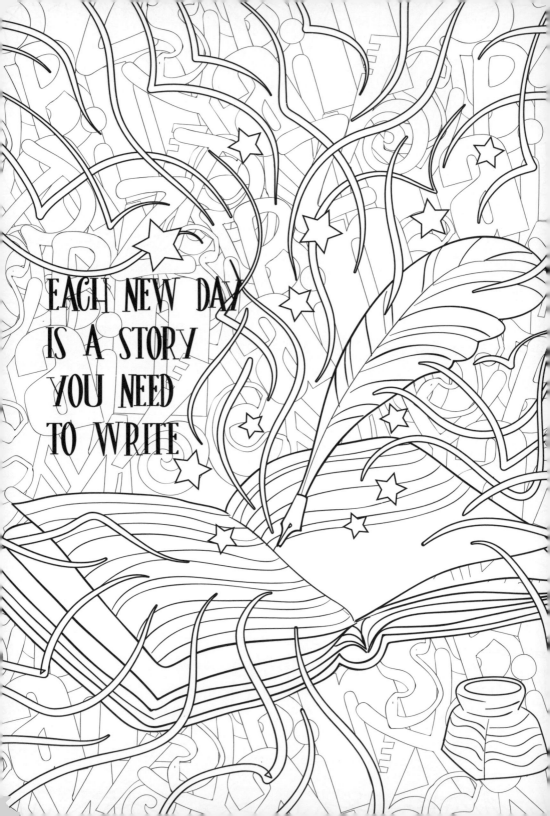

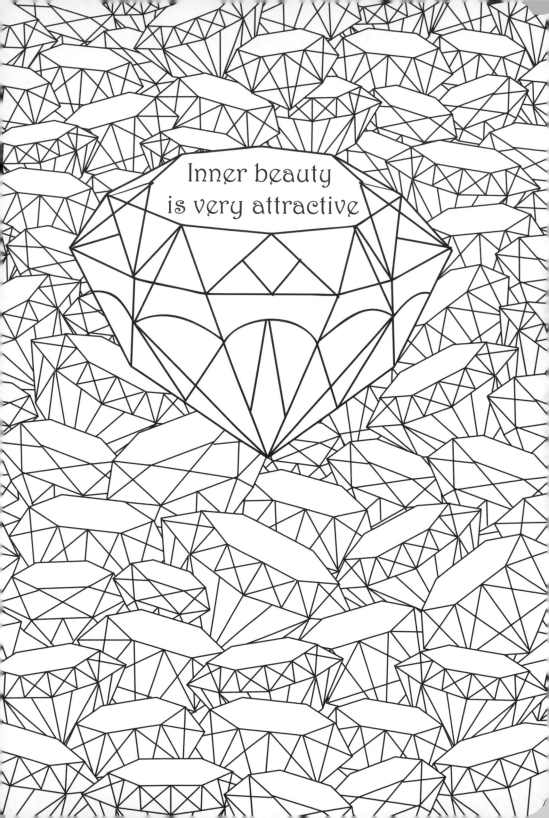

Inner beauty
is very attractive

MAKE YOUR ACTIONS BIGGER
THAN YOUR EXCUSES

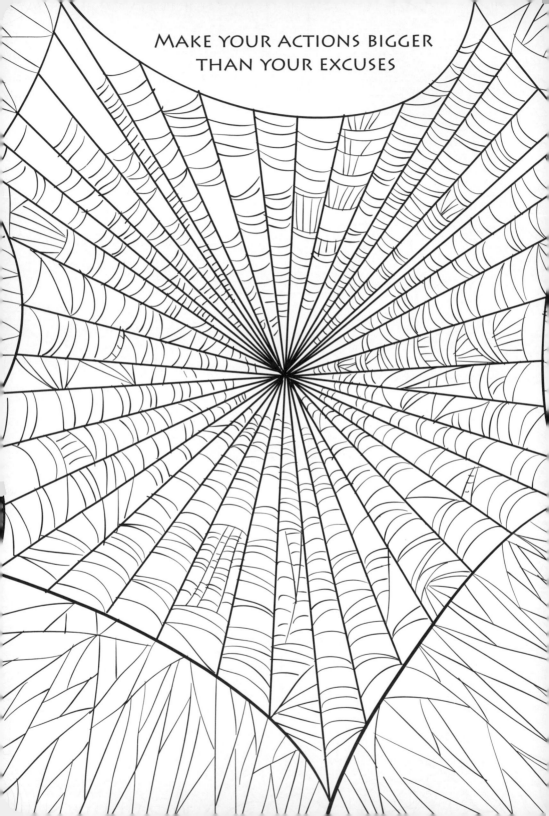

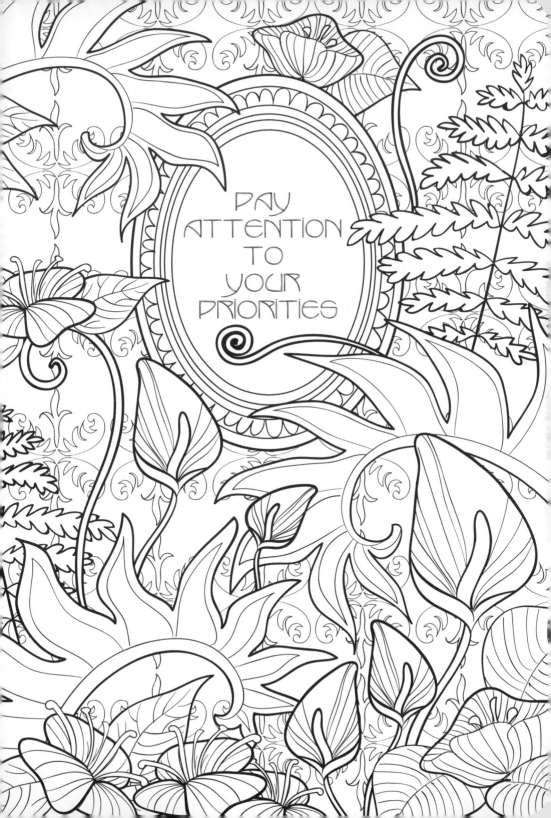

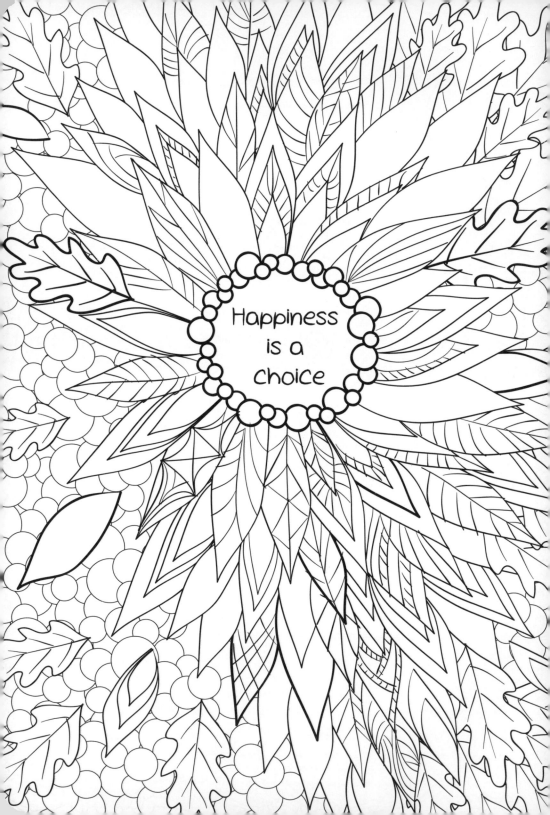

Happiness
is a
choice

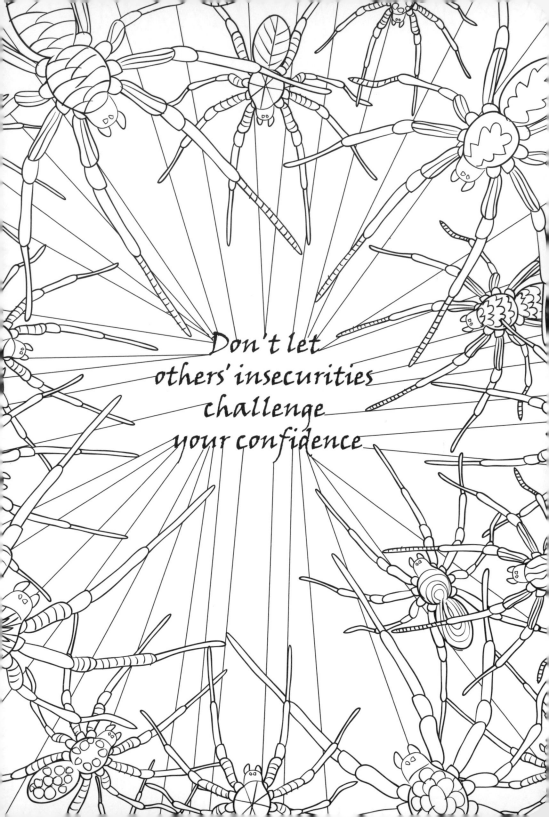

Don't let
others' insecurities
challenge
your confidence

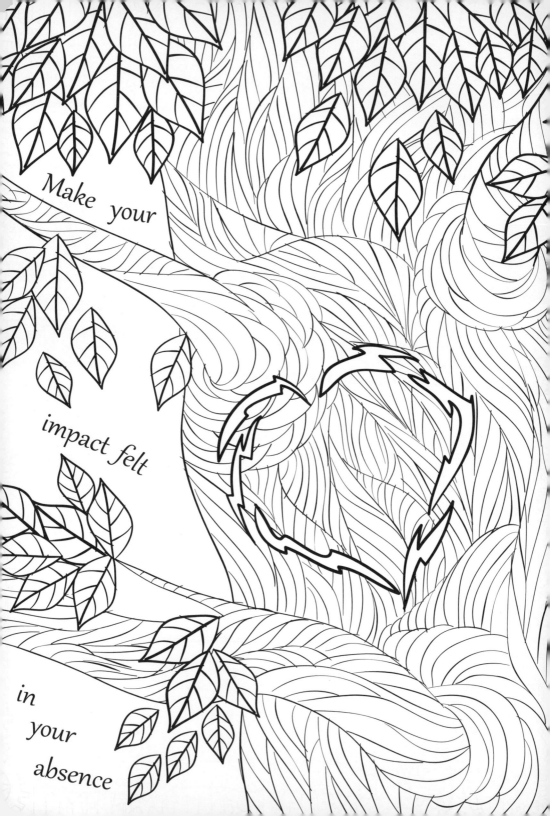

Make your

impact felt

in

your

absence

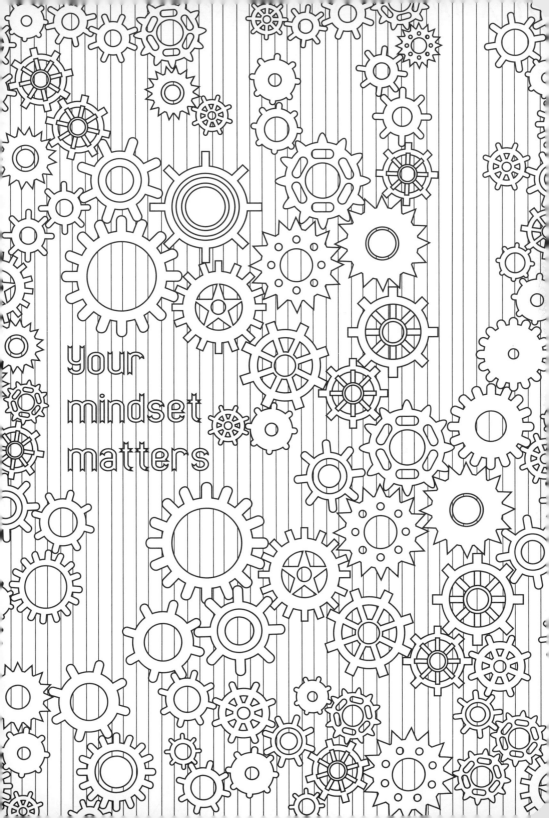

your mindset matters

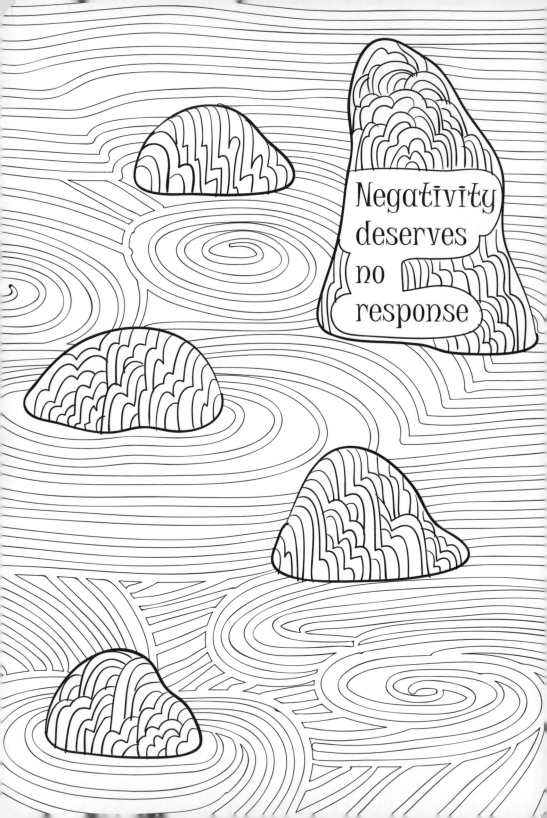

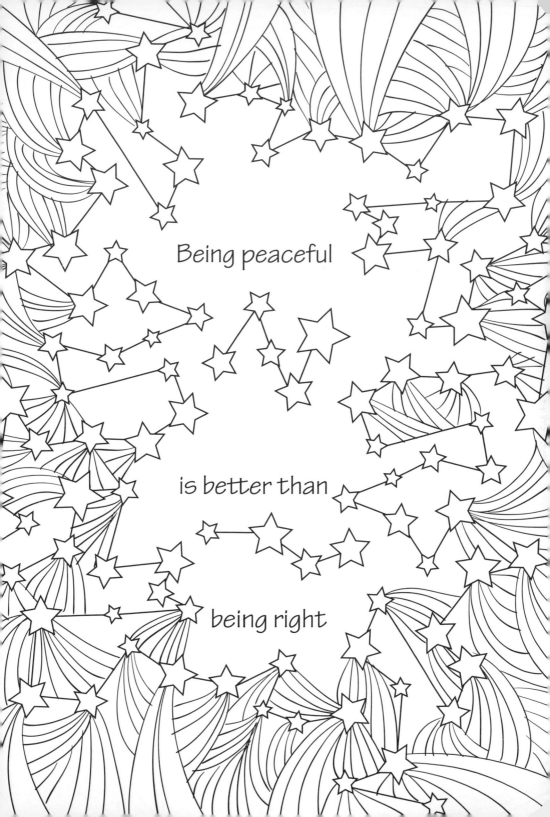

Being peaceful

is better than

being right

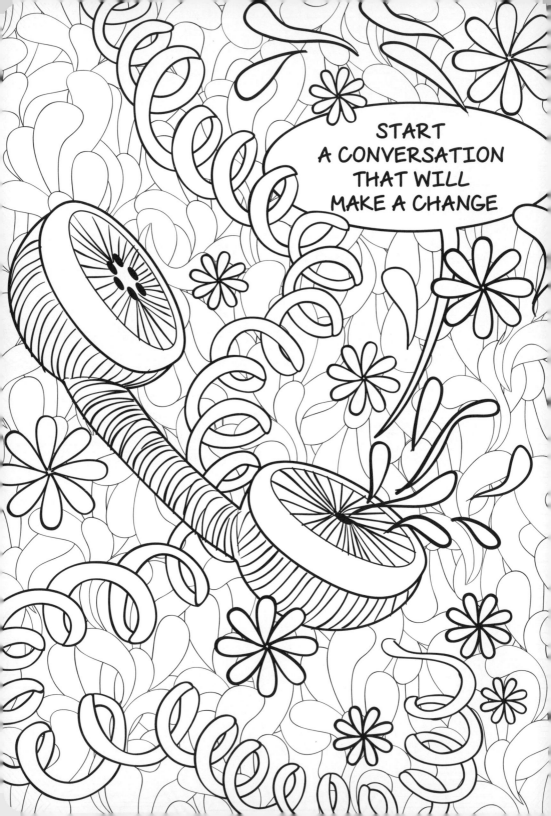

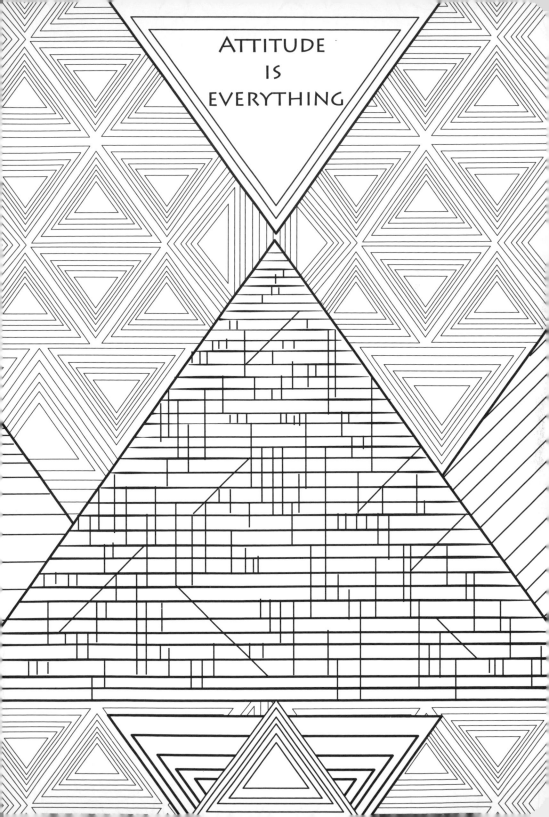

ATTITUDE
IS
EVERYTHING

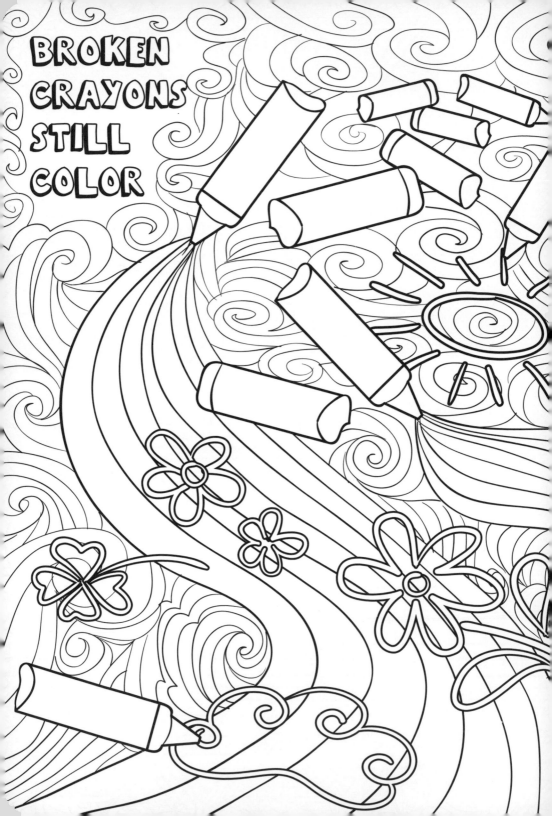

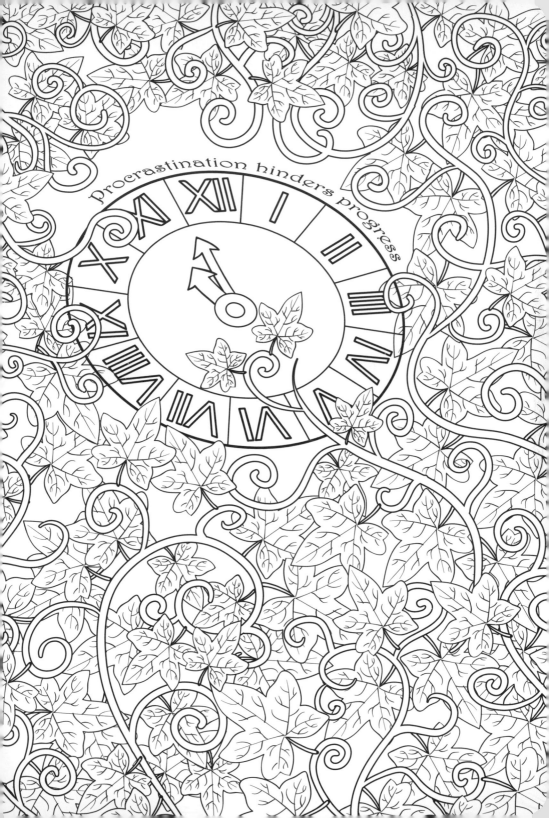

procrastination hinders progress

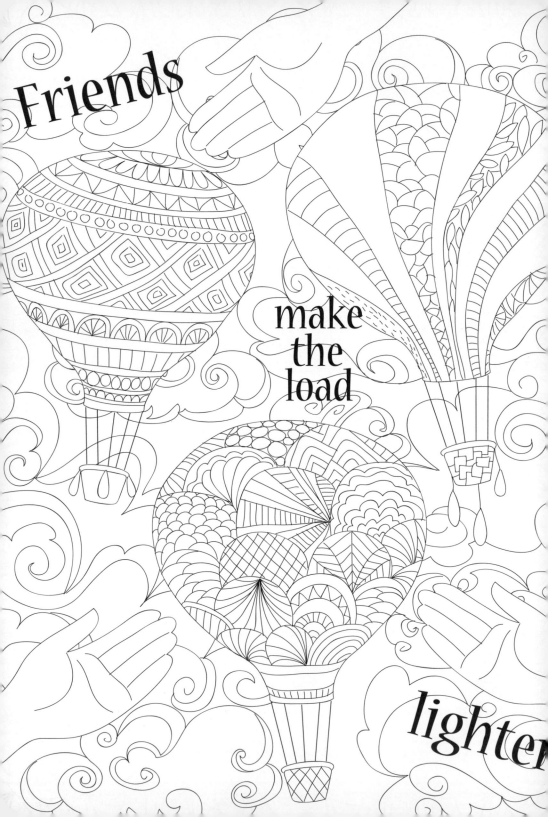

Friends

make
the
load

lighter

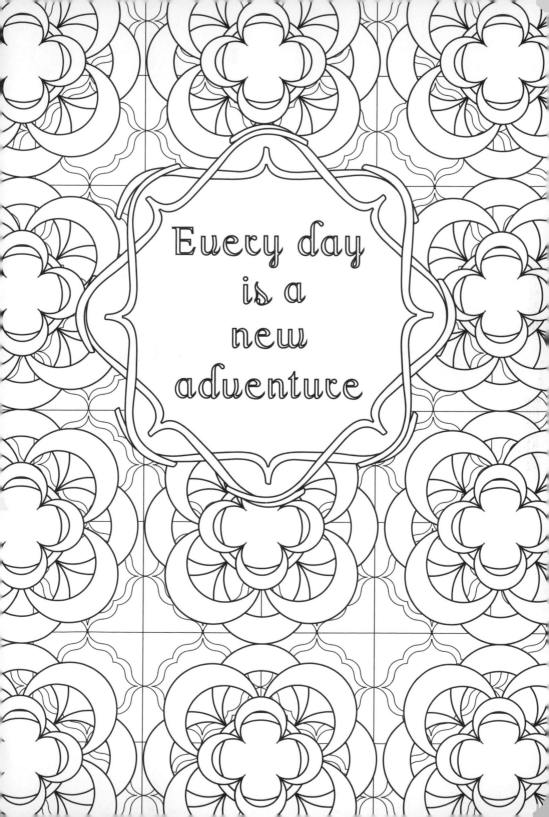

Every day
is a
new
adventure

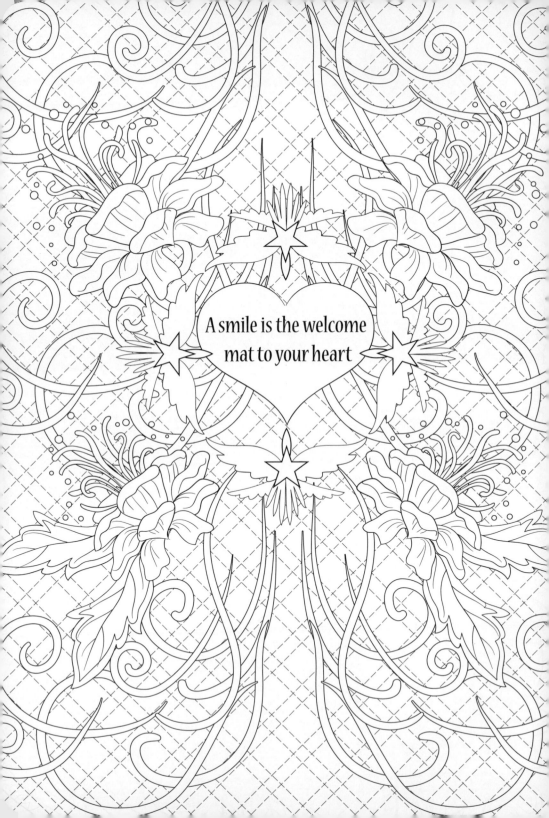

A smile is the welcome
mat to your heart

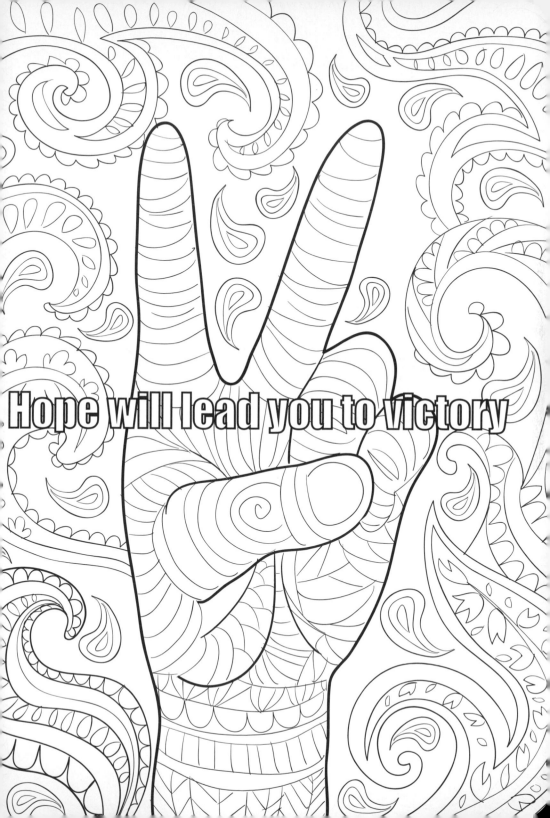

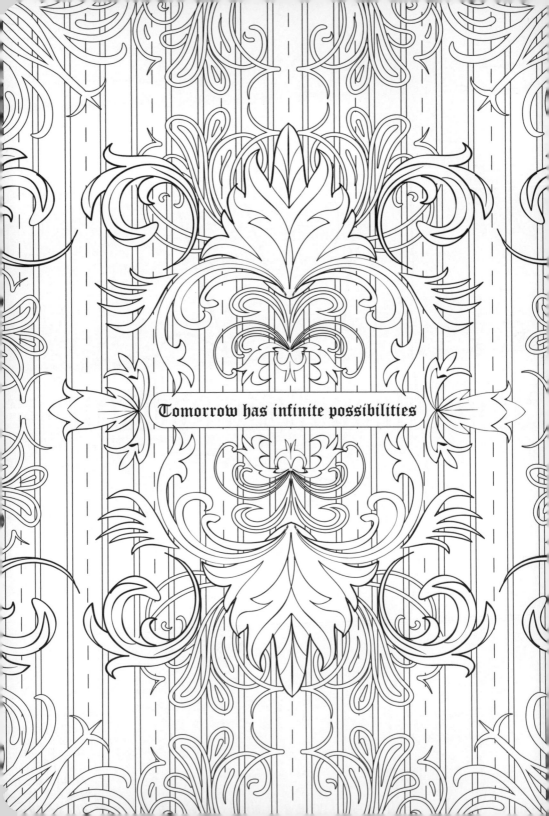

Tomorrow has infinite possibilities

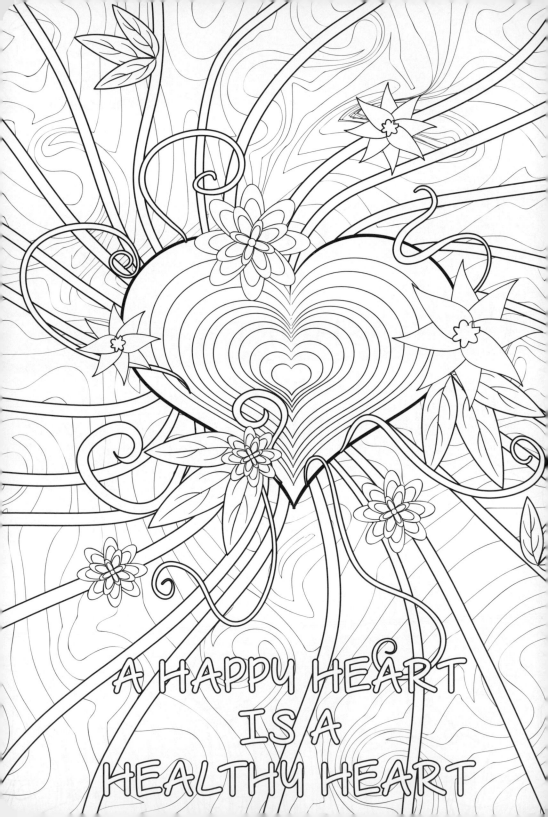

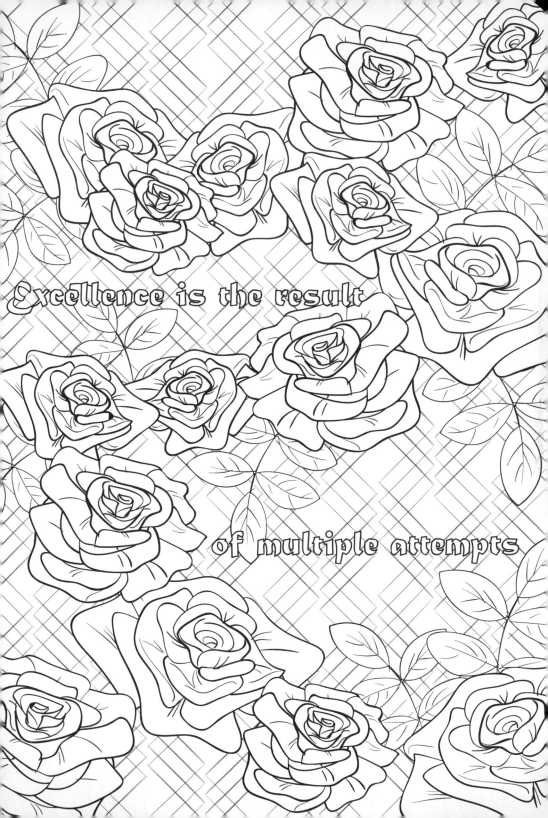

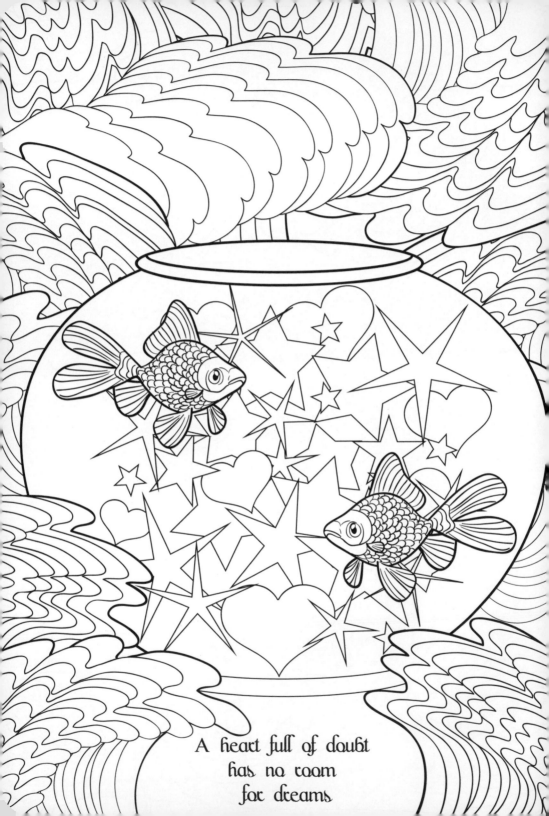

A heart full of doubt
has no room
for dreams

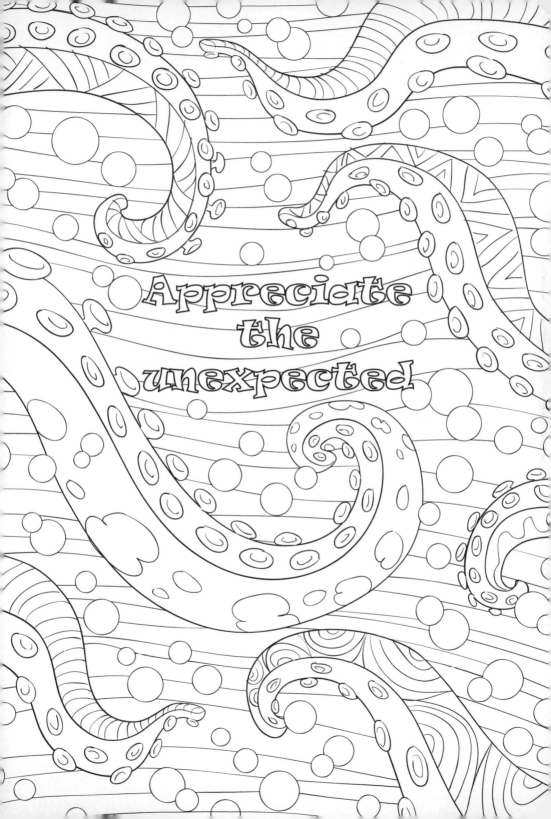

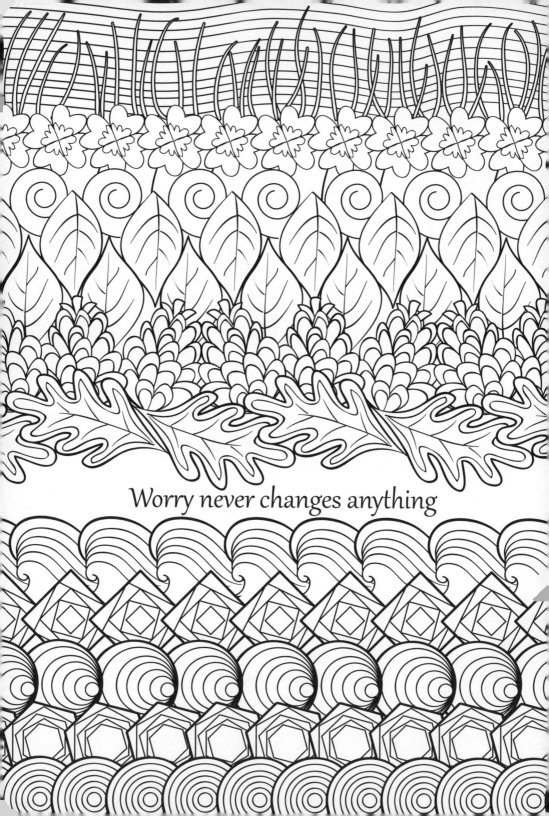

Worry never changes anything

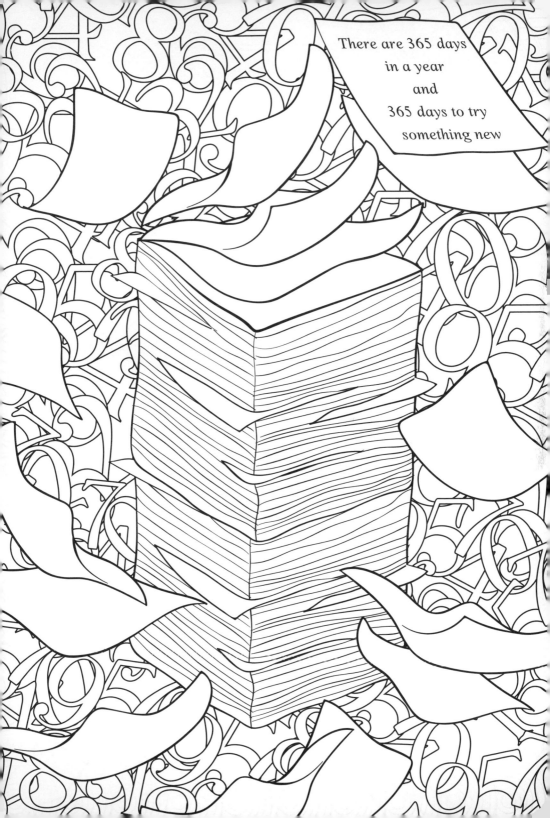

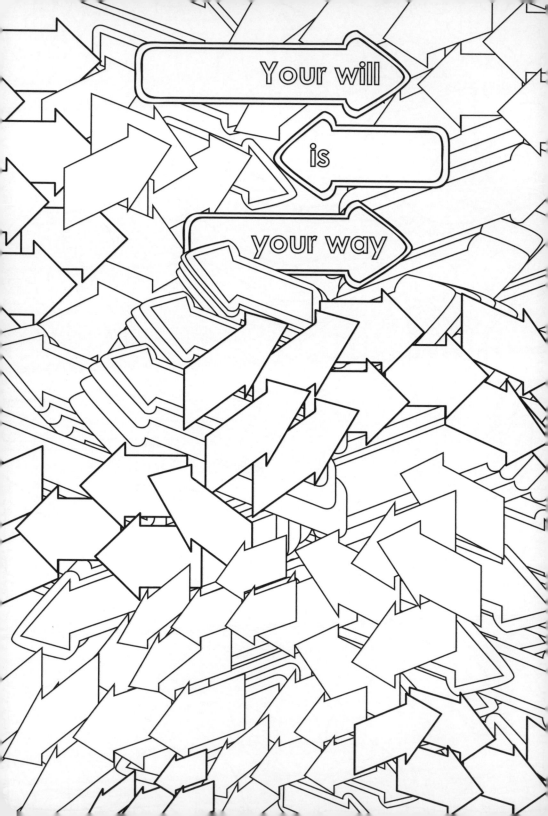

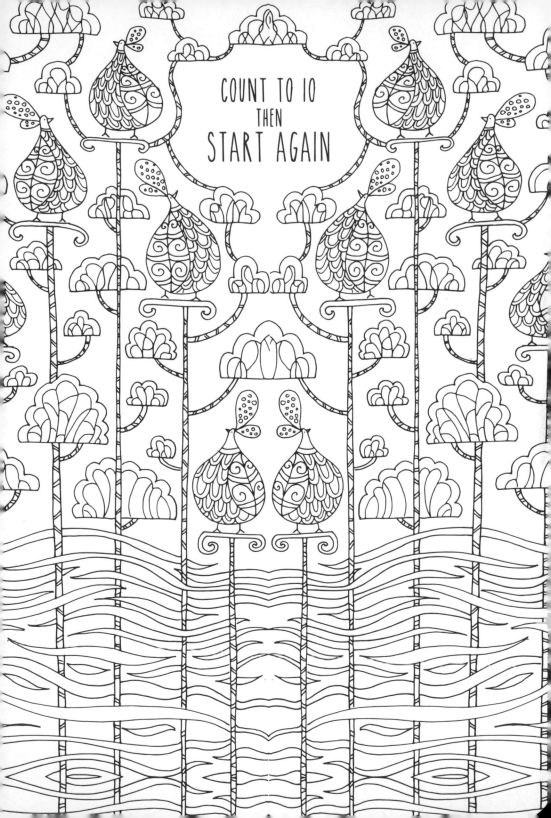

COUNT TO 10
THEN
START AGAIN

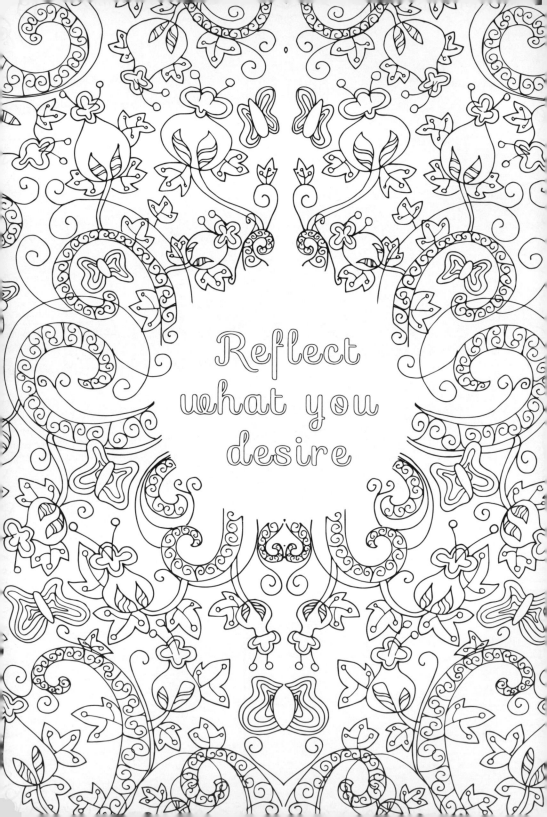

Reflect
what you
desire

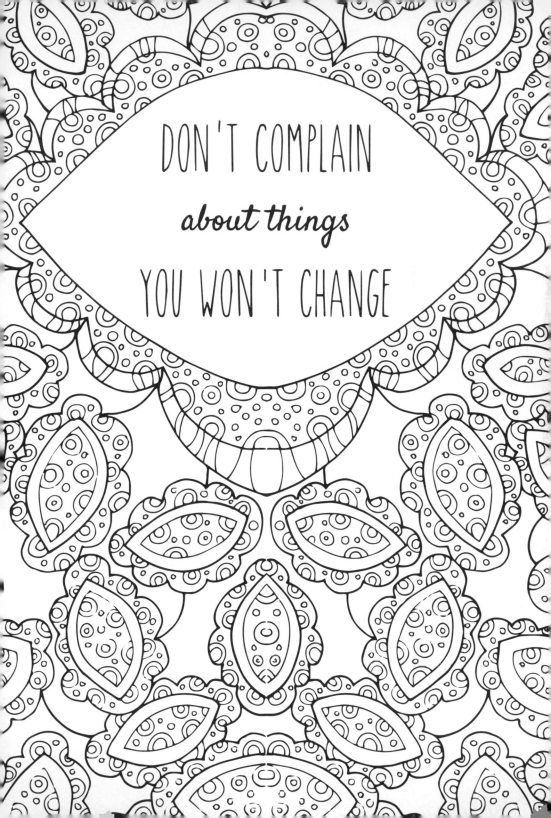

DON'T COMPLAIN
about things
YOU WON'T CHANGE

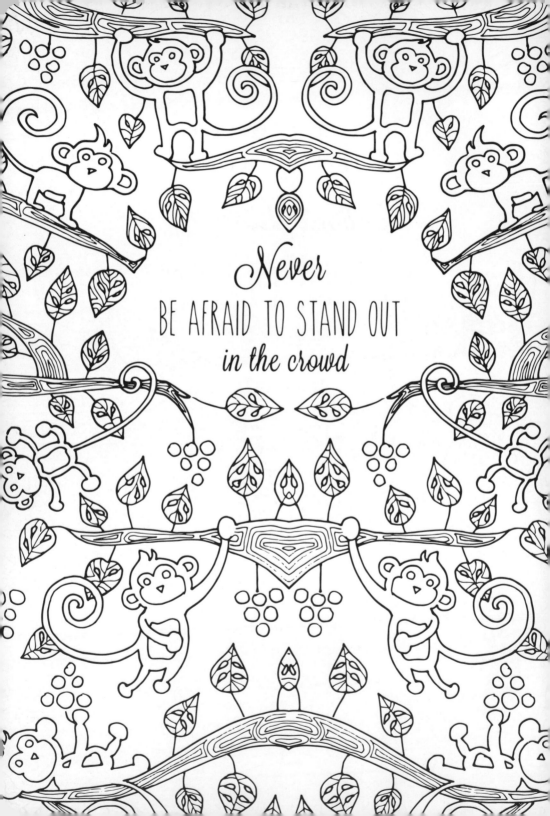

Never
BE AFRAID TO STAND OUT
in the crowd

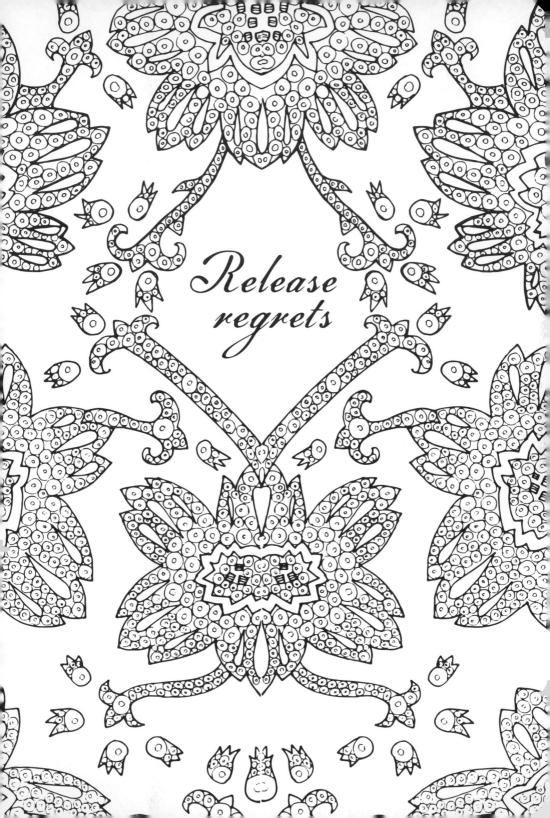

Release
regrets

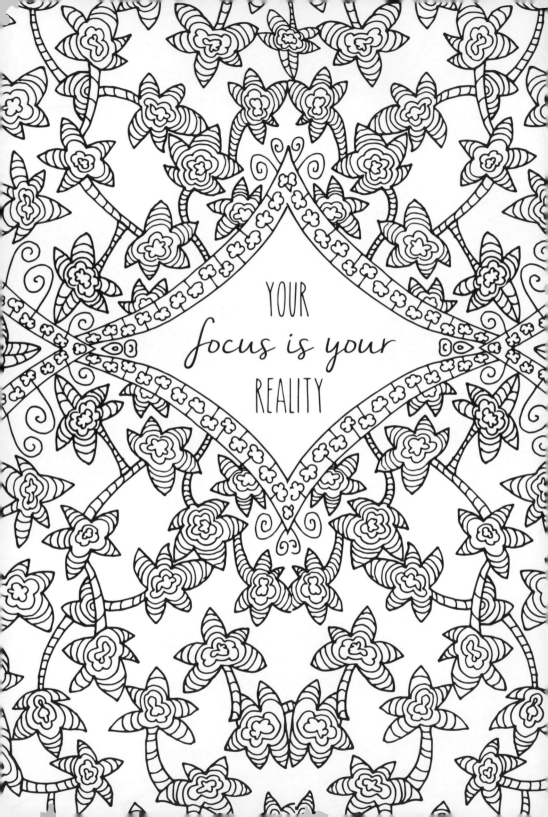

YOUR

focus is your

REALITY

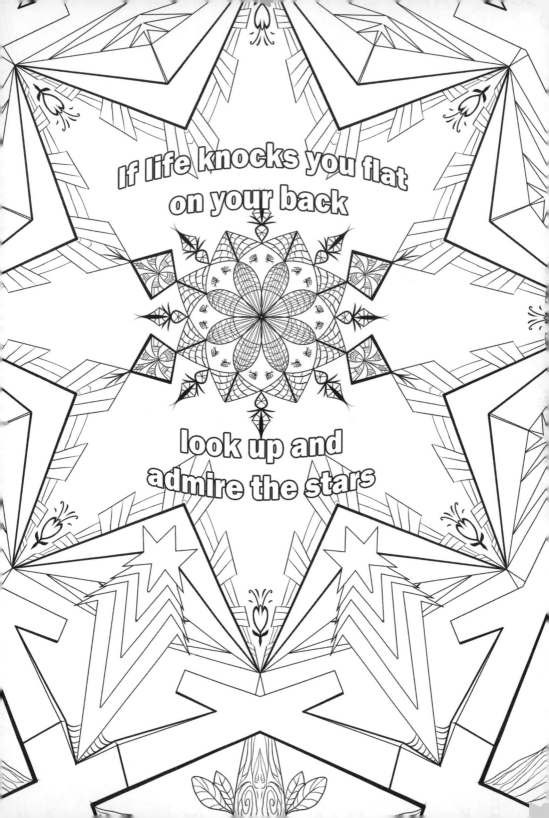

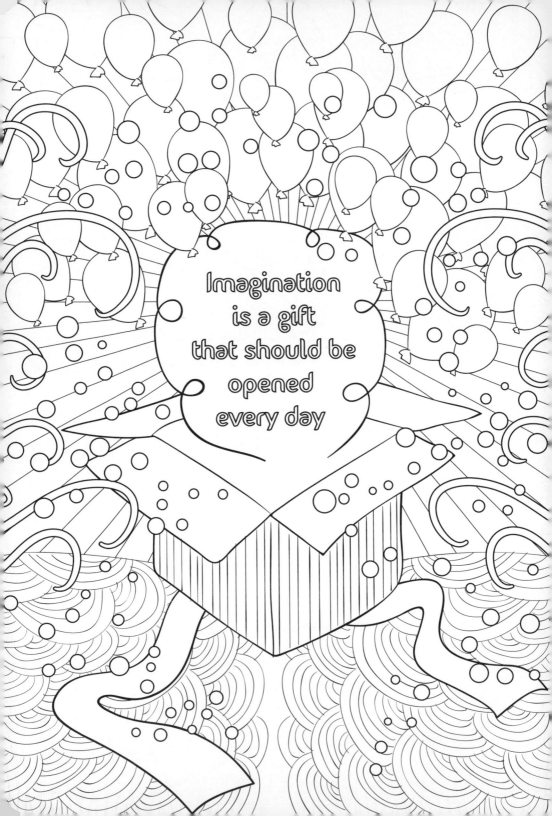

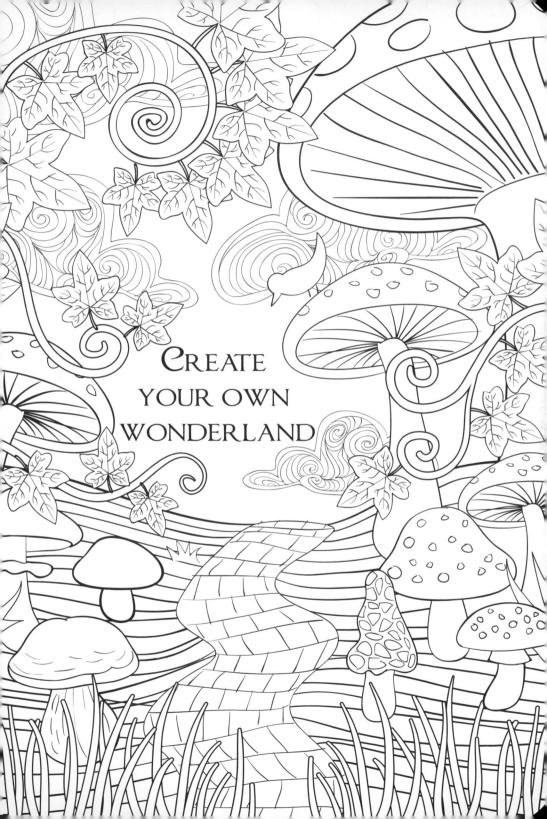

CREATE YOUR OWN WONDERLAND

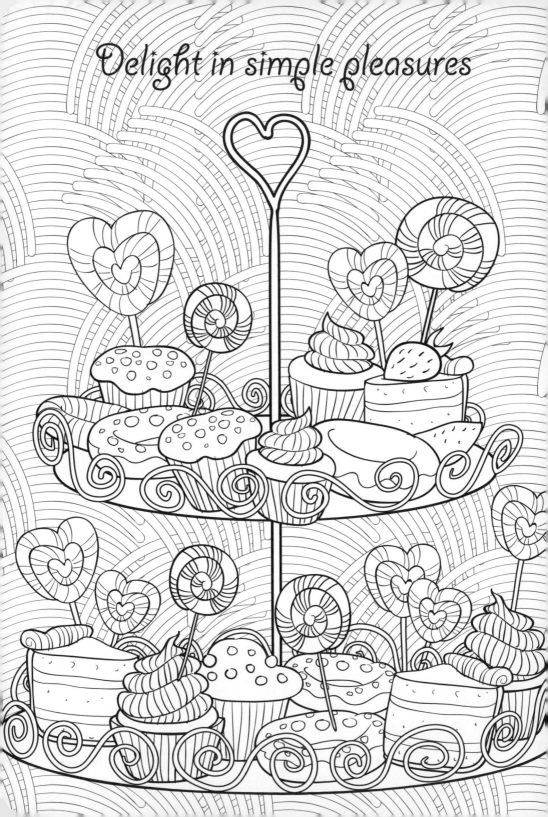

Delight in simple pleasures

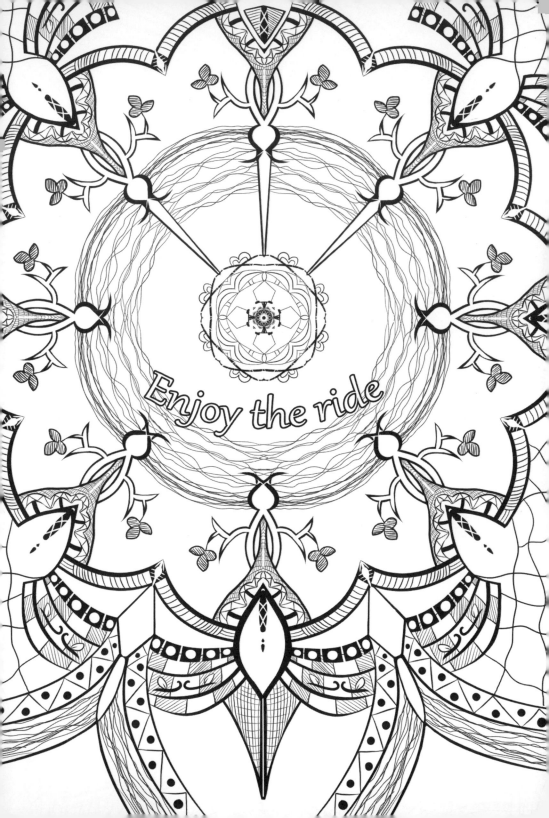

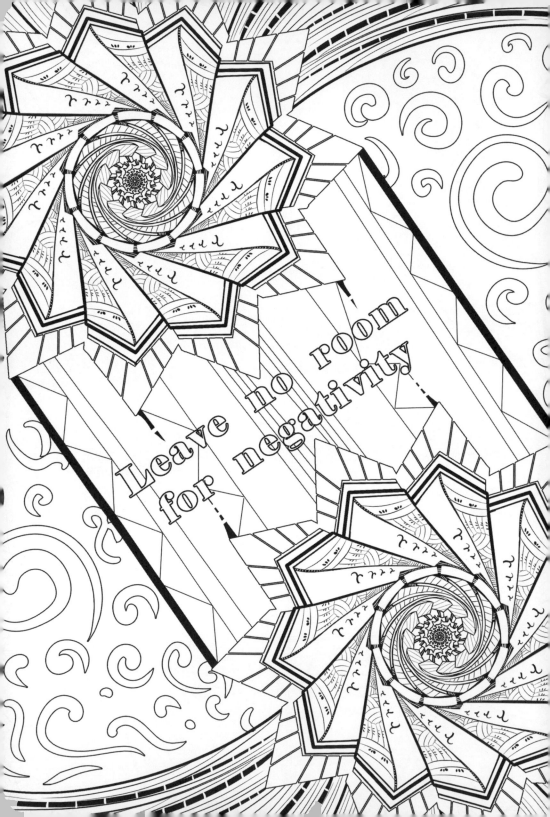

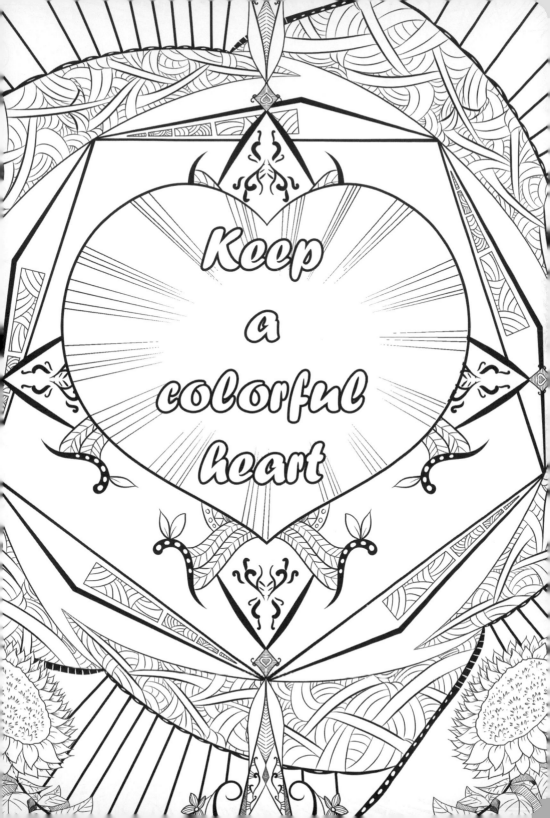

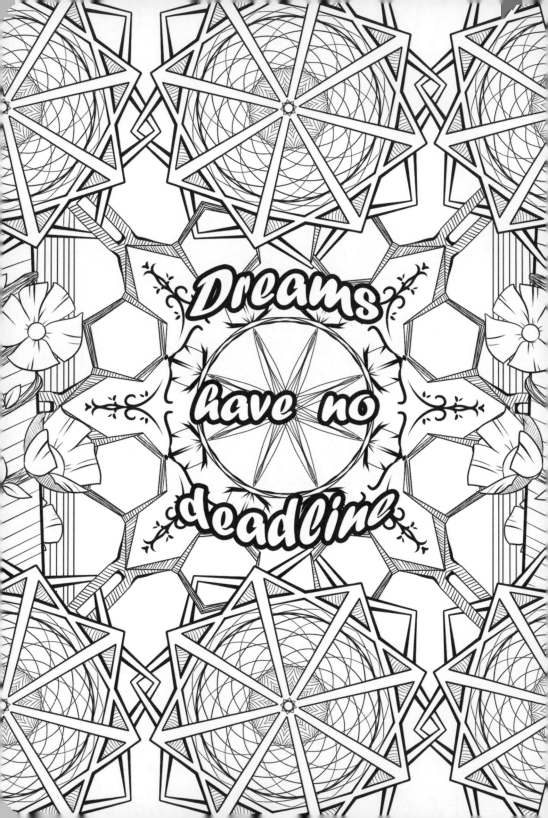

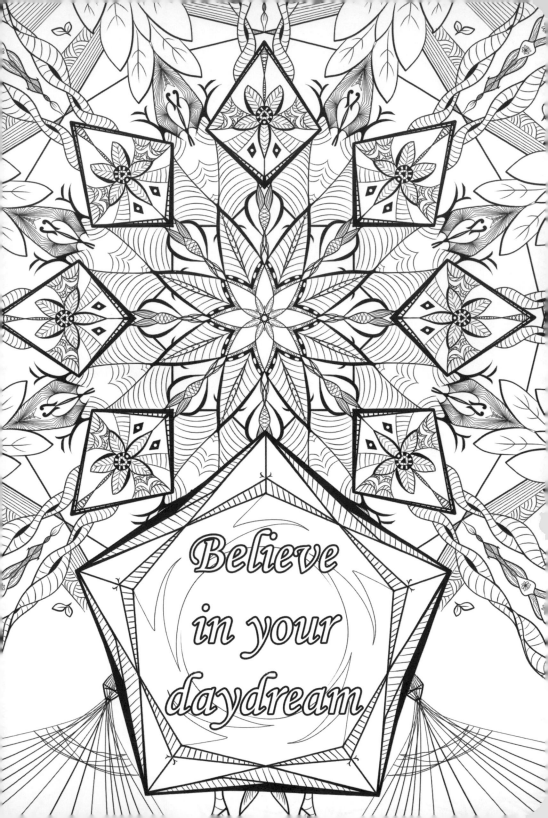

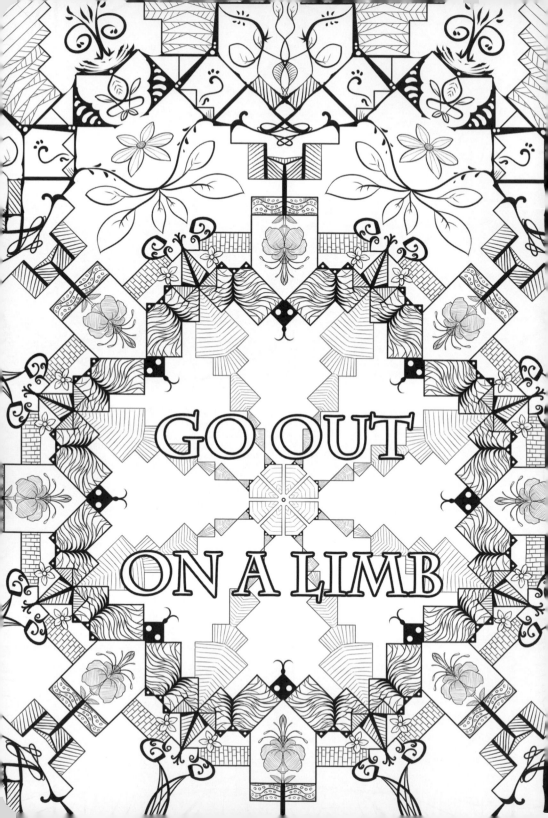

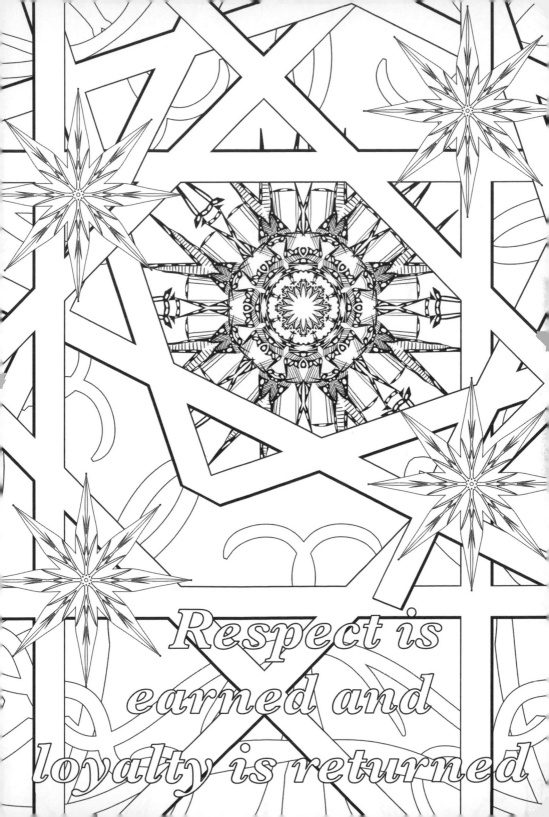

Respect is earned and loyalty is returned

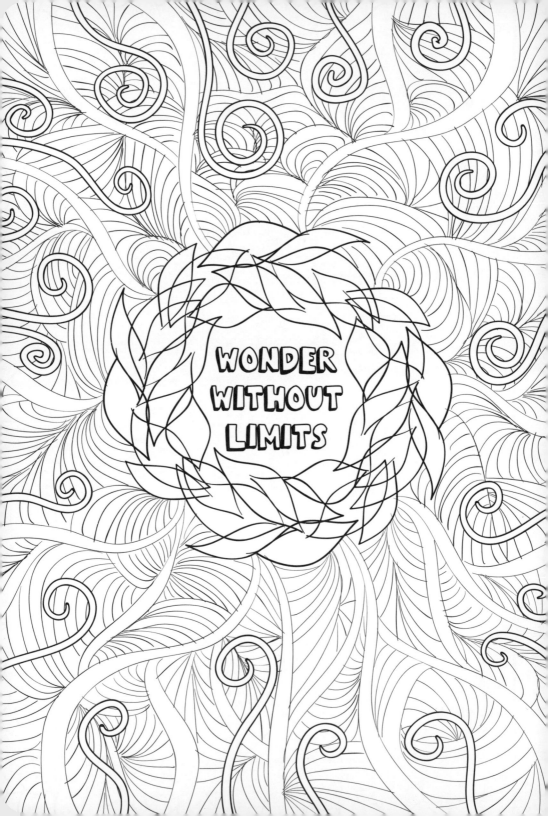

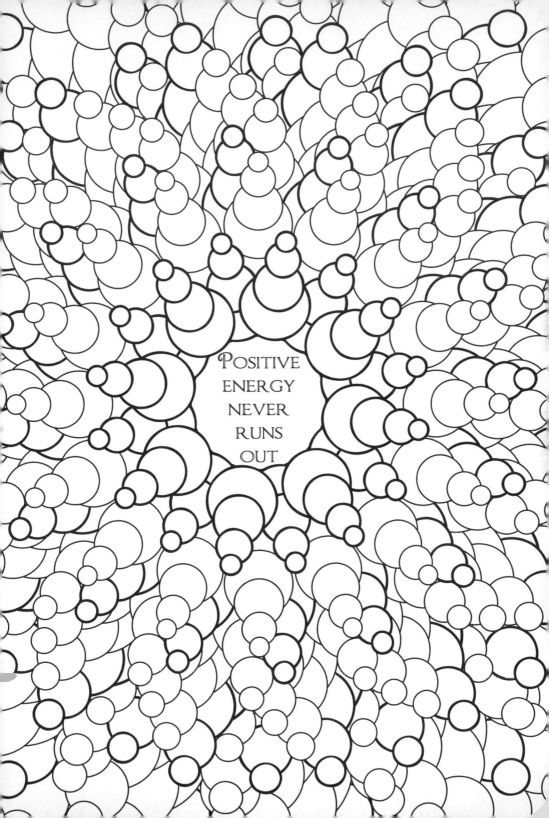

Positive
energy
never
runs
out

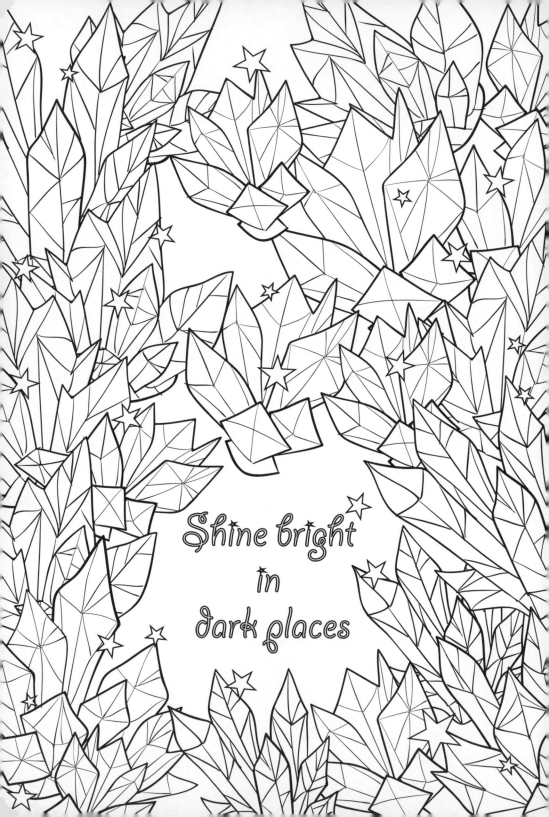

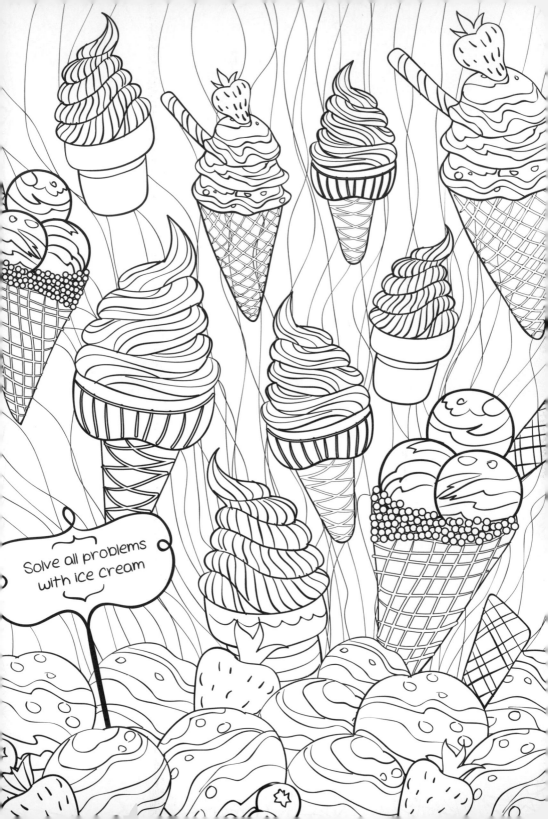

Solve all problems with ice cream

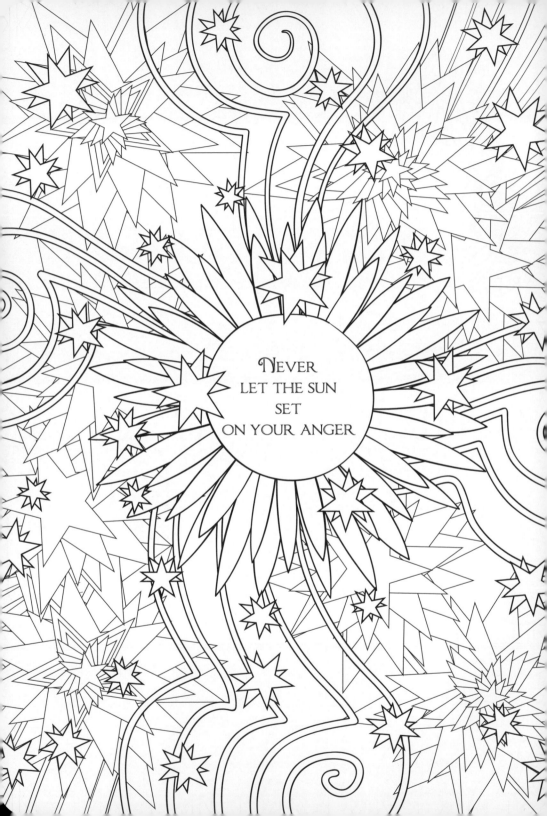

Never
let the sun
set
on your anger

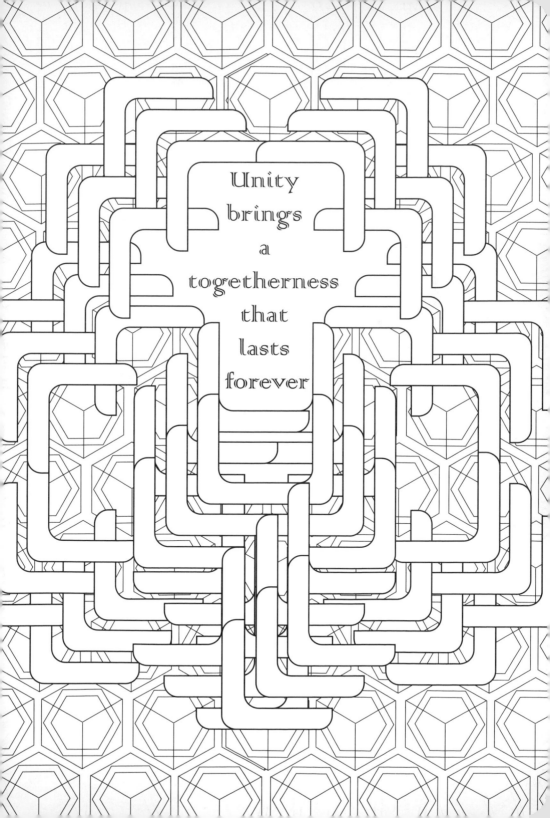

Unity
brings
a
togetherness
that
lasts
forever

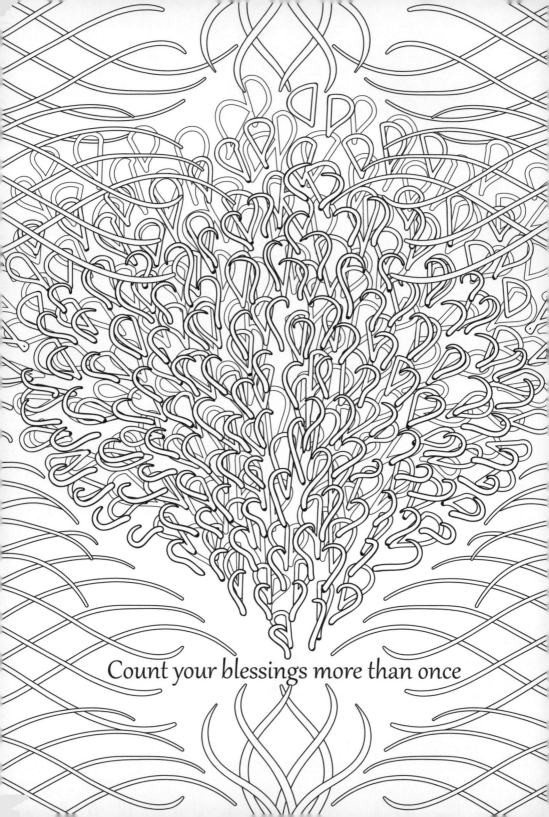

Count your blessings more than once

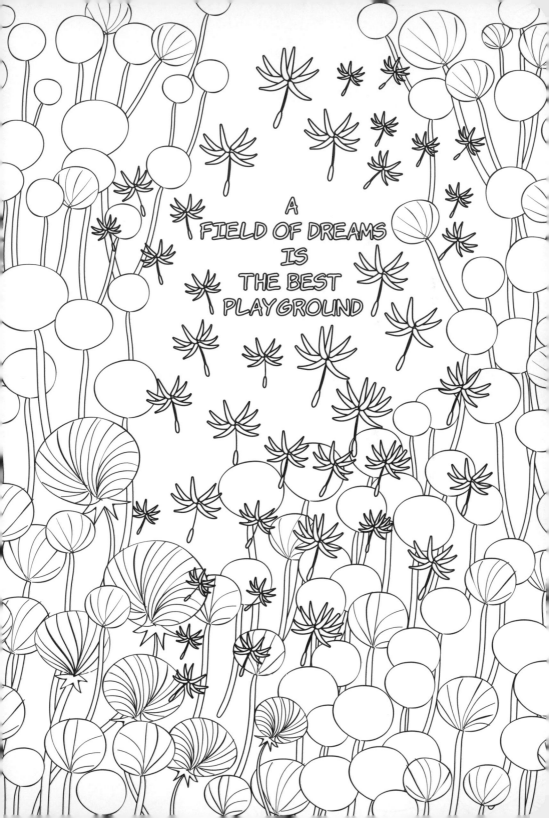

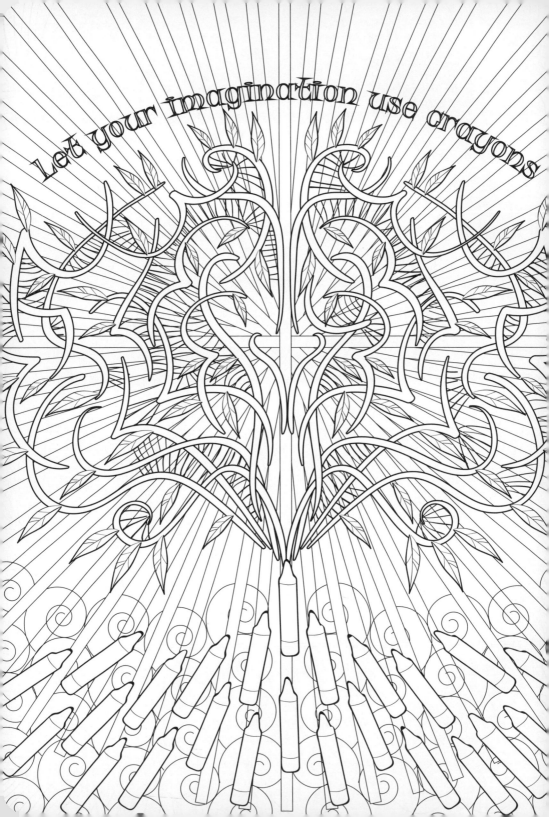

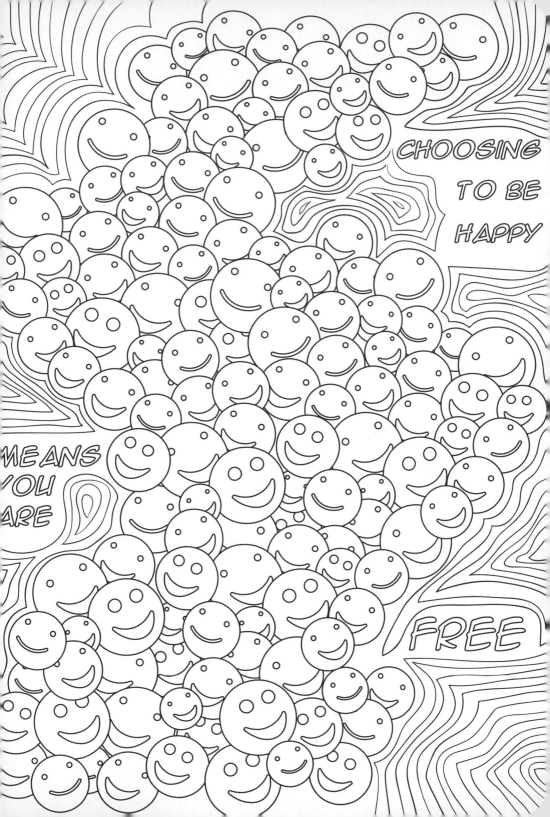

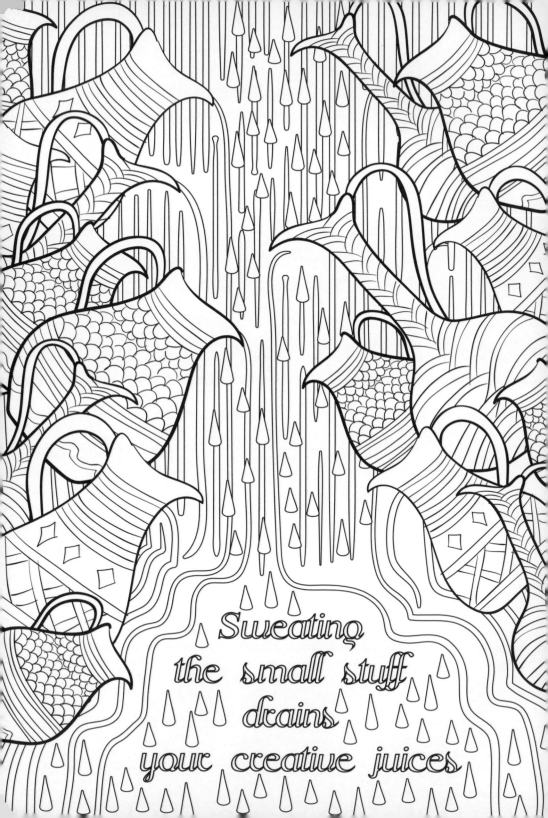

Sweating
the small stuff
drains
your creative juices

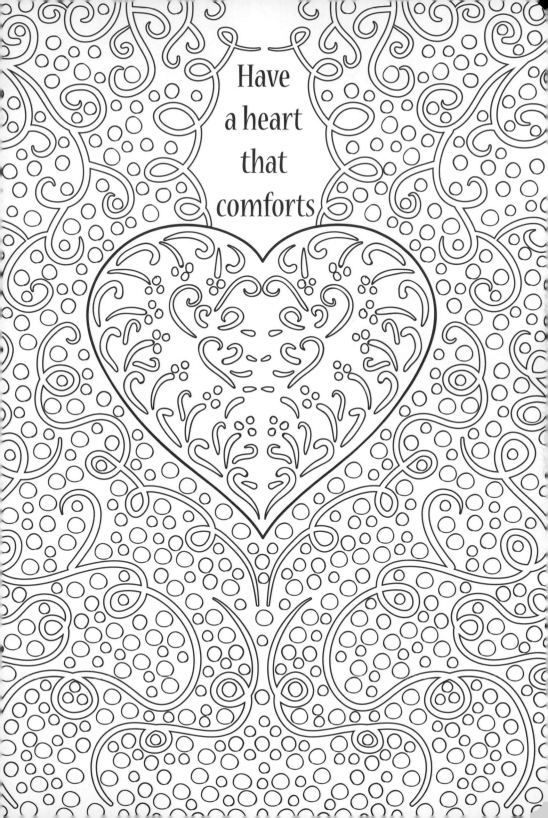

Have
a heart
that
comforts

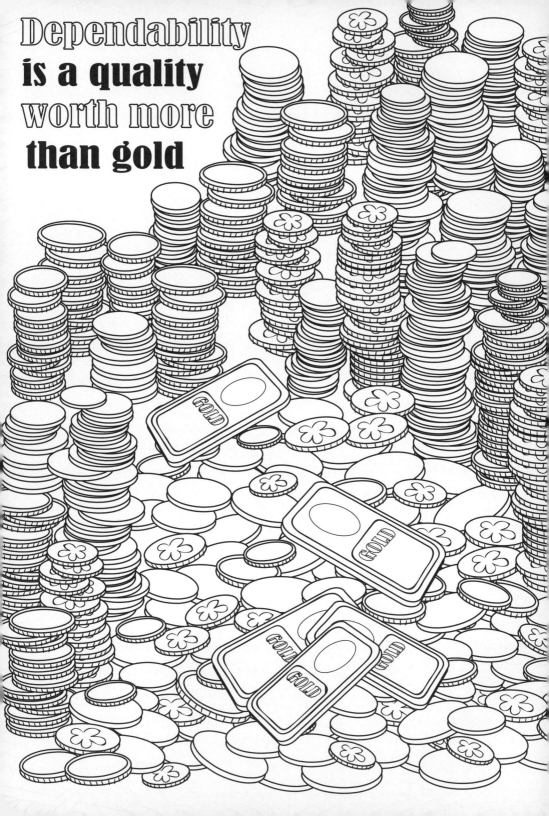

Dependability is a quality worth more than gold

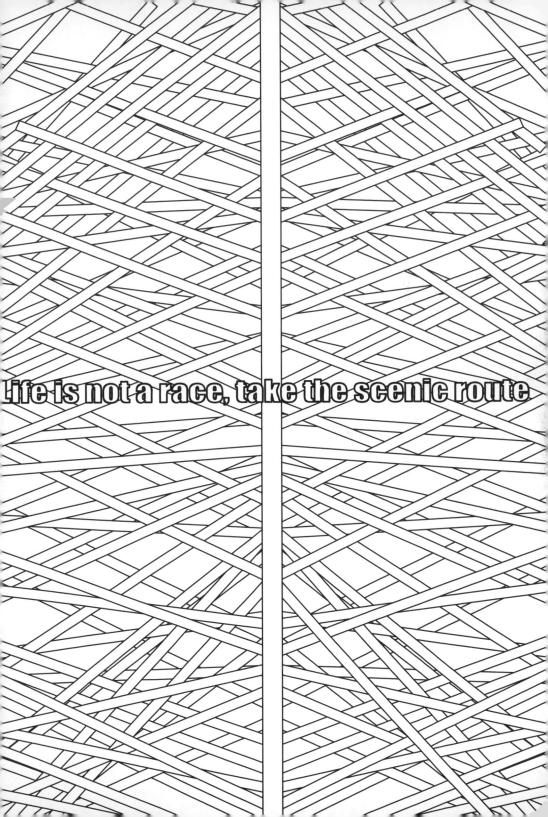

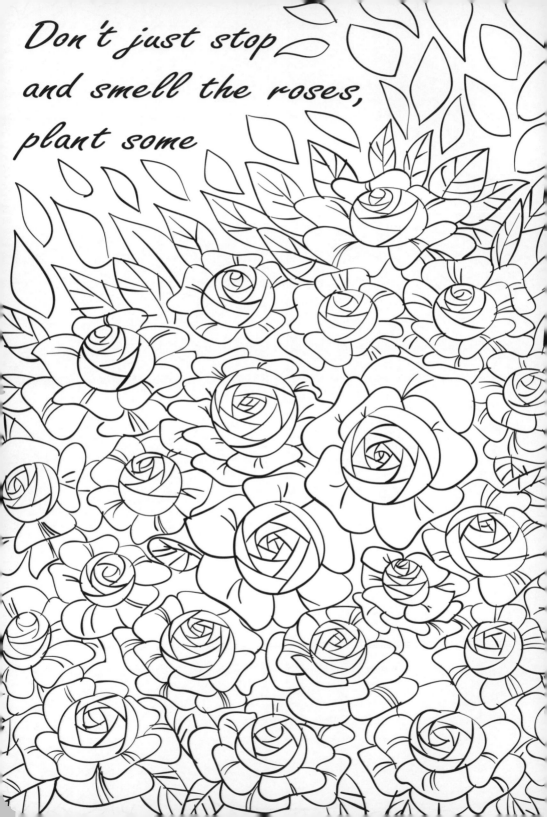
Don't just stop and smell the roses, plant some

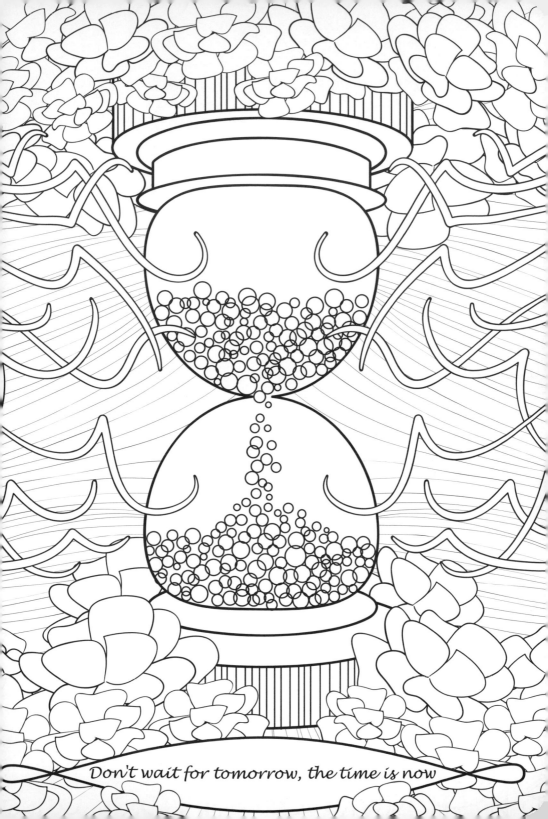

Don't wait for tomorrow, the time is now

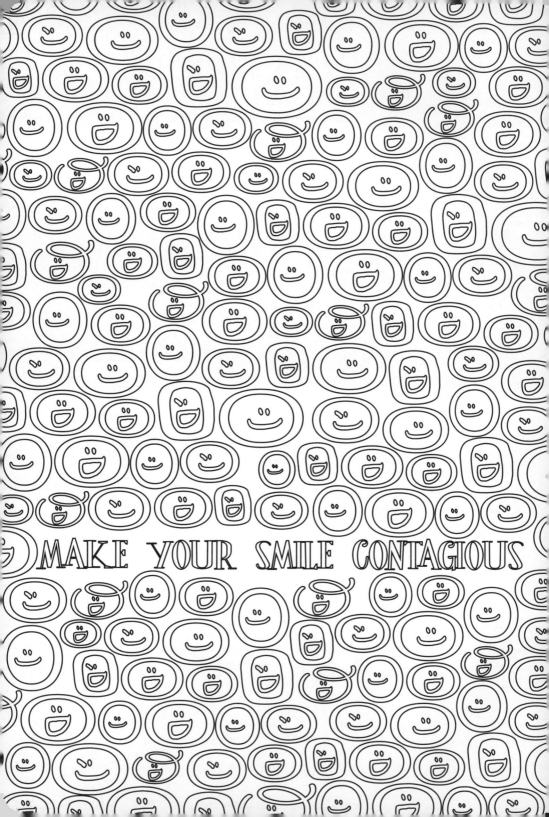

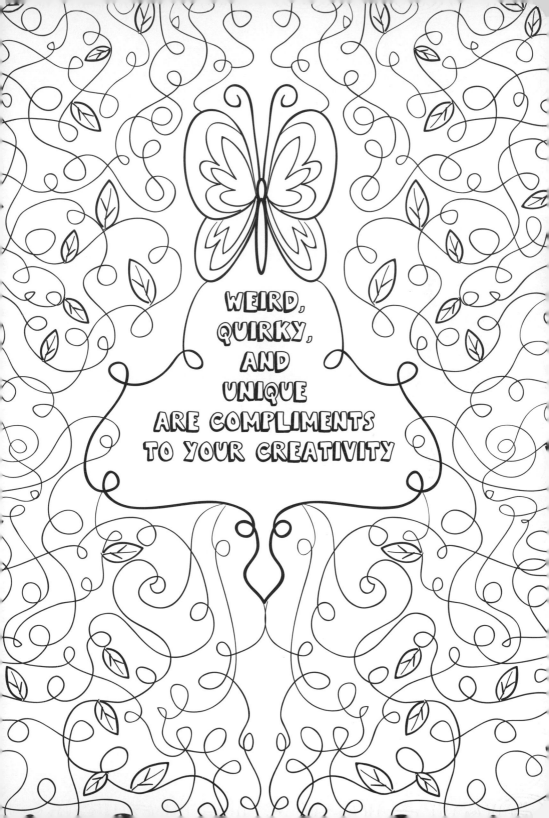

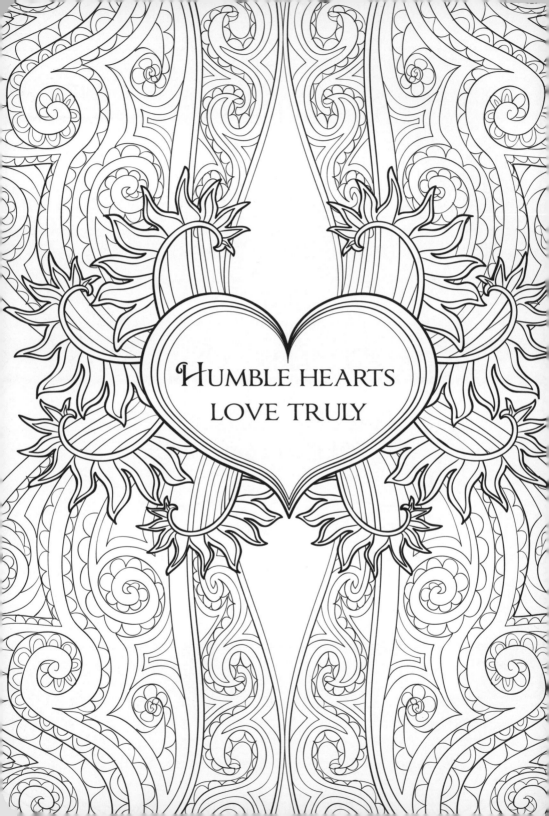

HUMBLE HEARTS
LOVE TRULY

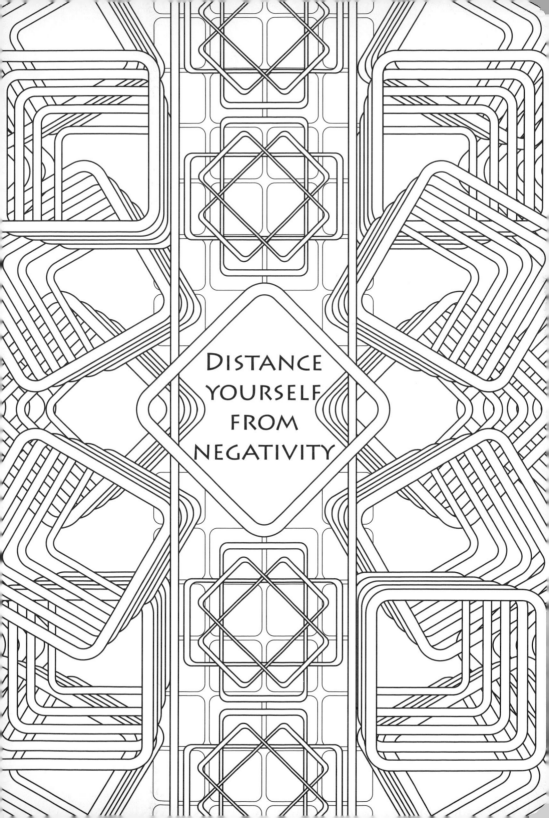

DISTANCE
YOURSELF
FROM
NEGATIVITY

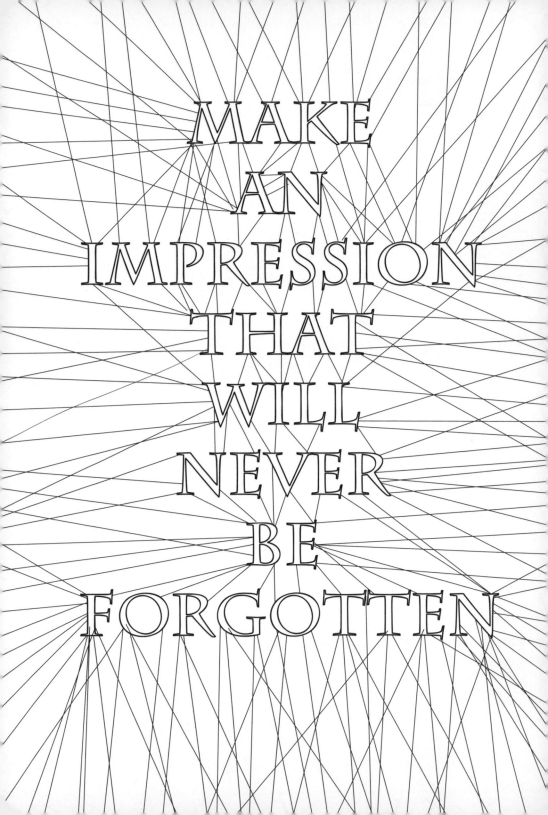

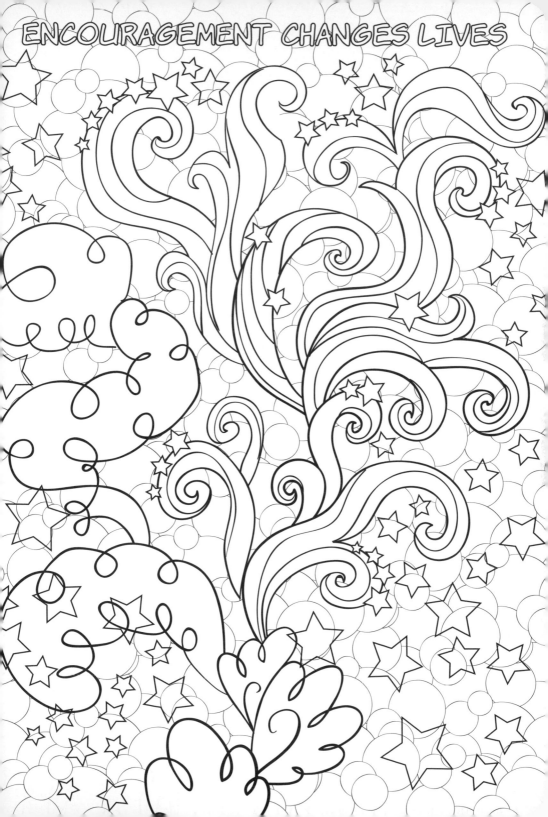

ENCOURAGEMENT CHANGES LIVES

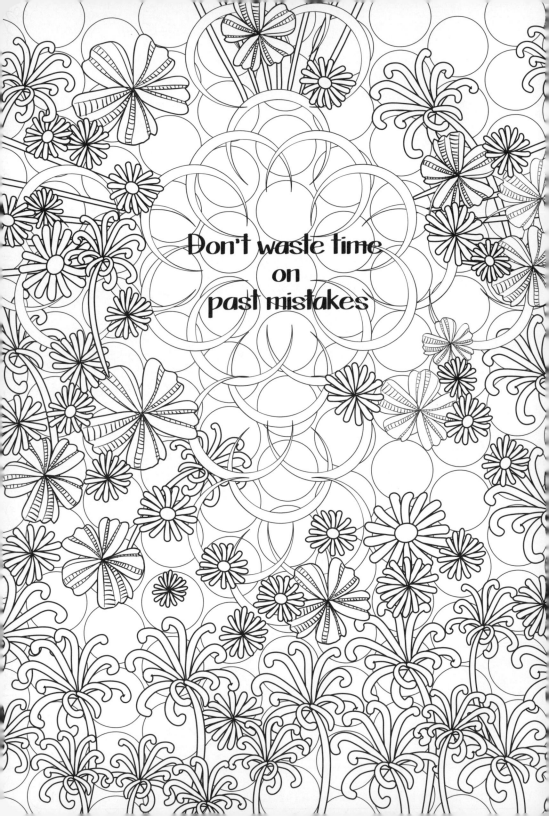

Don't waste time
on
past mistakes

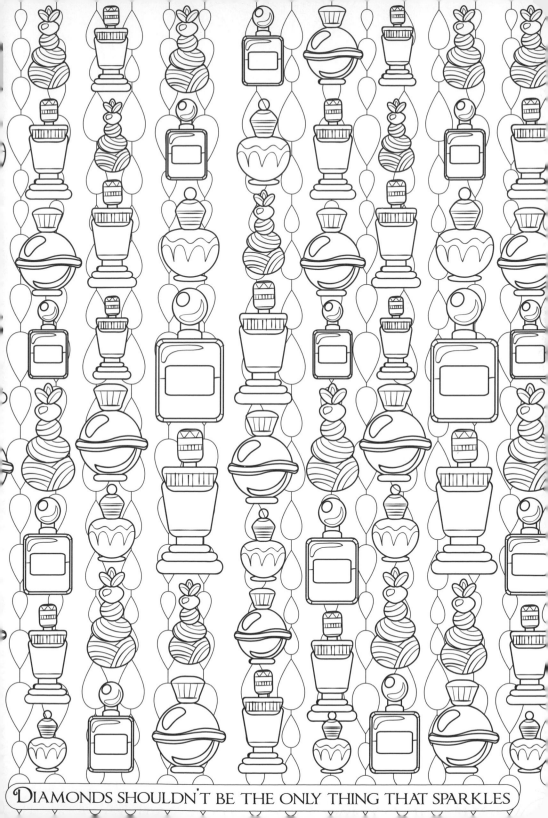

DIAMONDS SHOULDN'T BE THE ONLY THING THAT SPARKLES

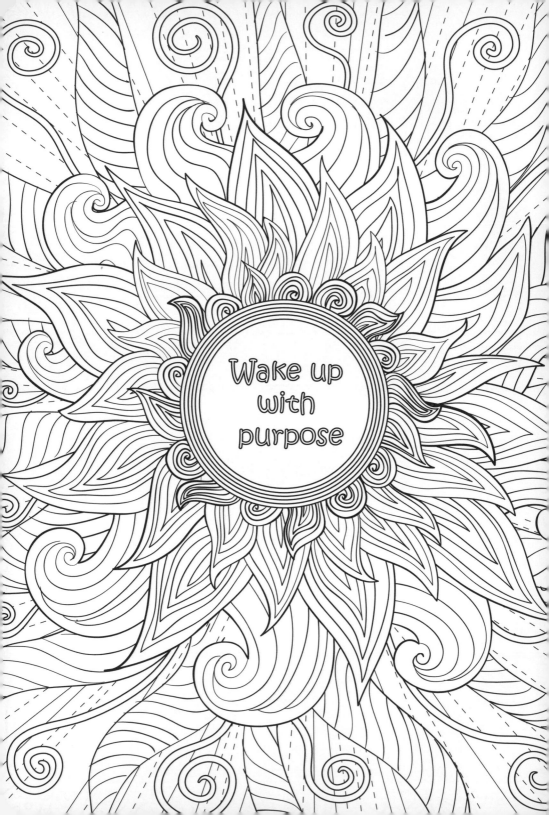

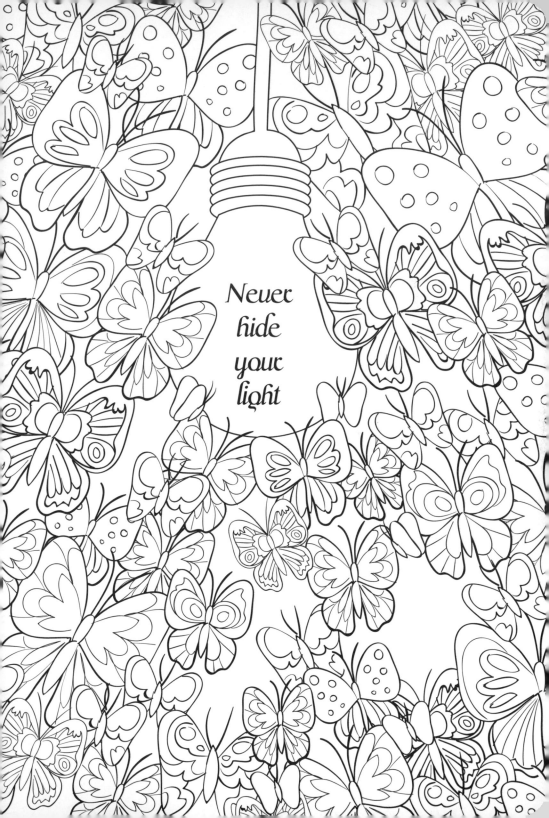

Never
hide
your
light

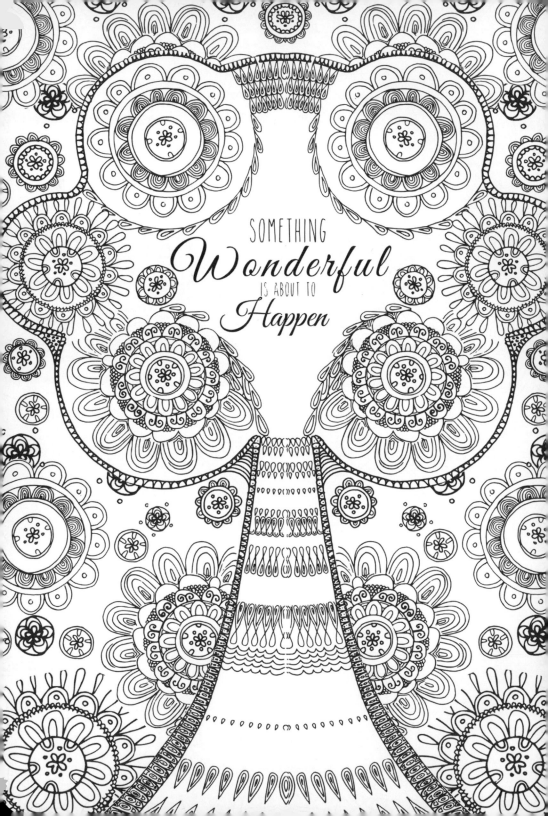

SOMETHING *Wonderful* IS ABOUT TO *Happen*

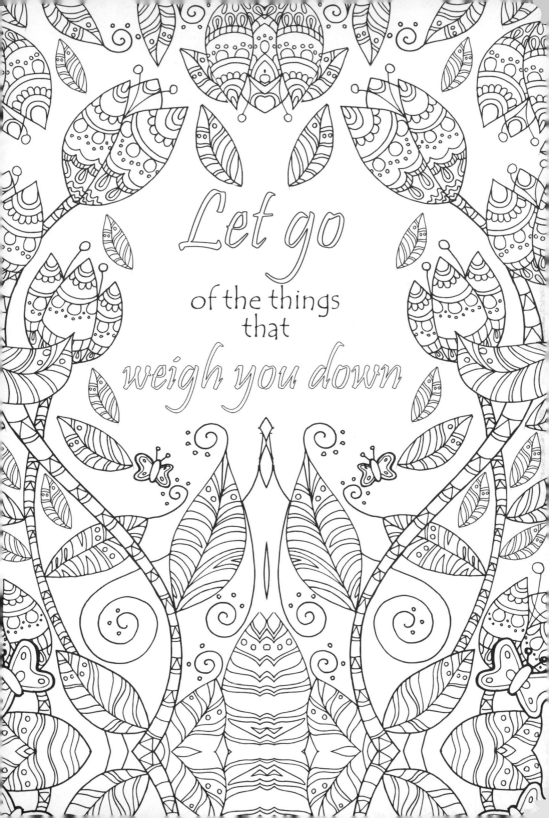

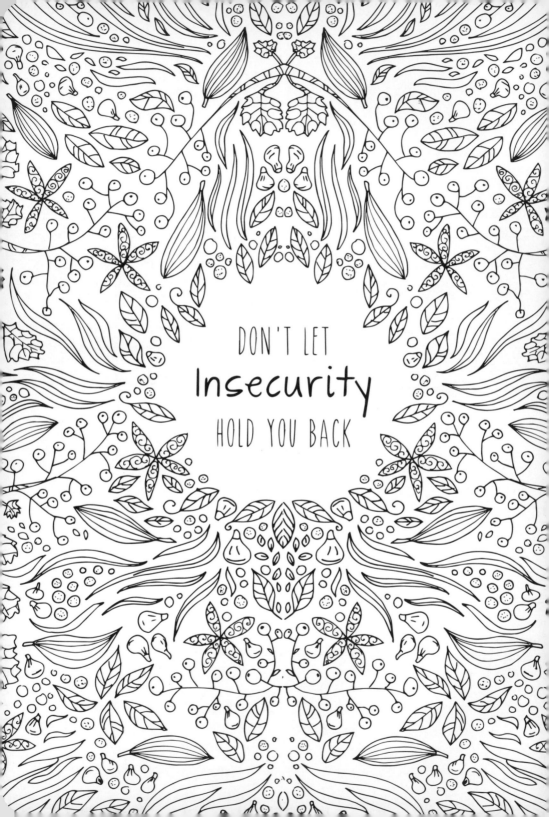

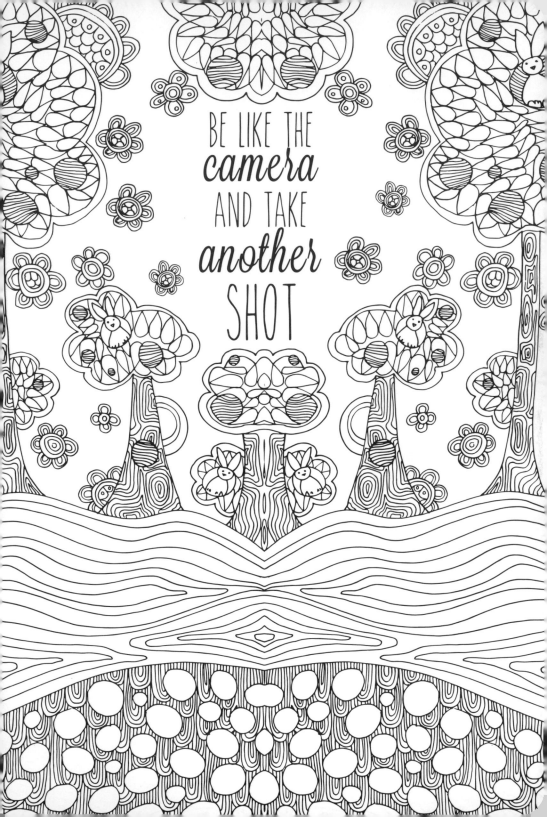

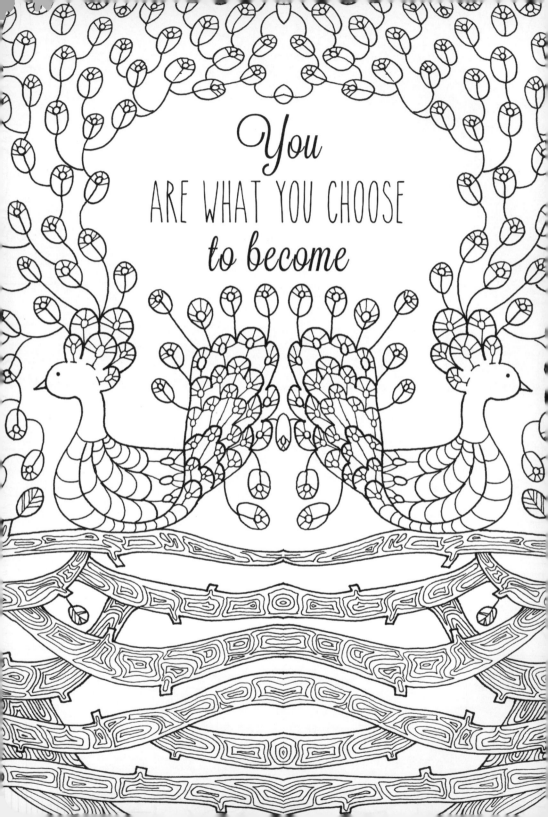

You
ARE WHAT YOU CHOOSE
to become

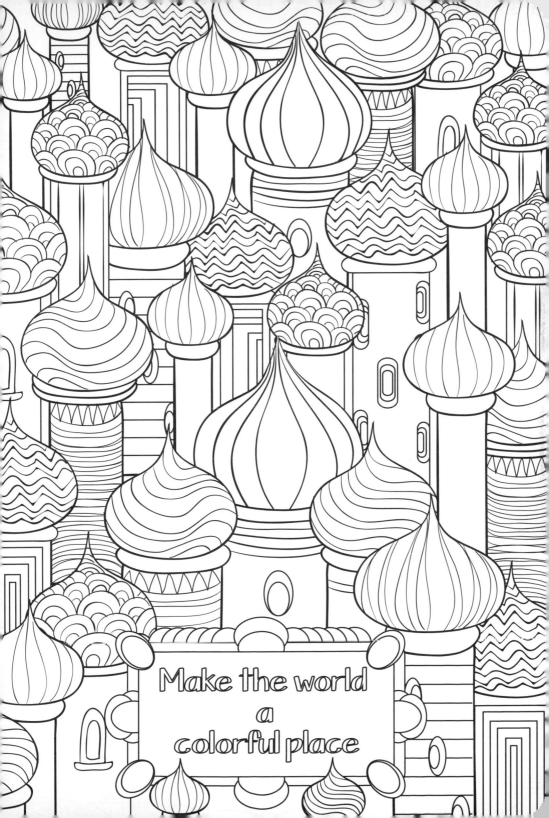

Make the world
a
colorful place

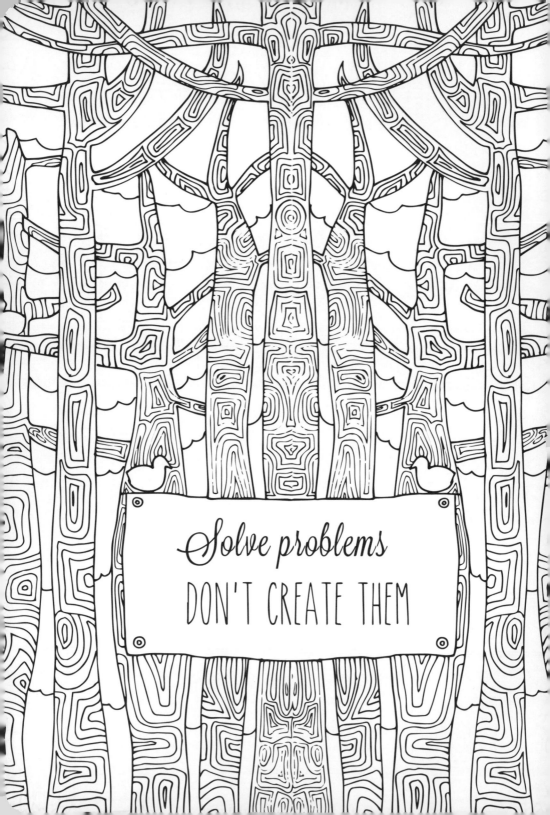

Solve problems
DON'T CREATE THEM

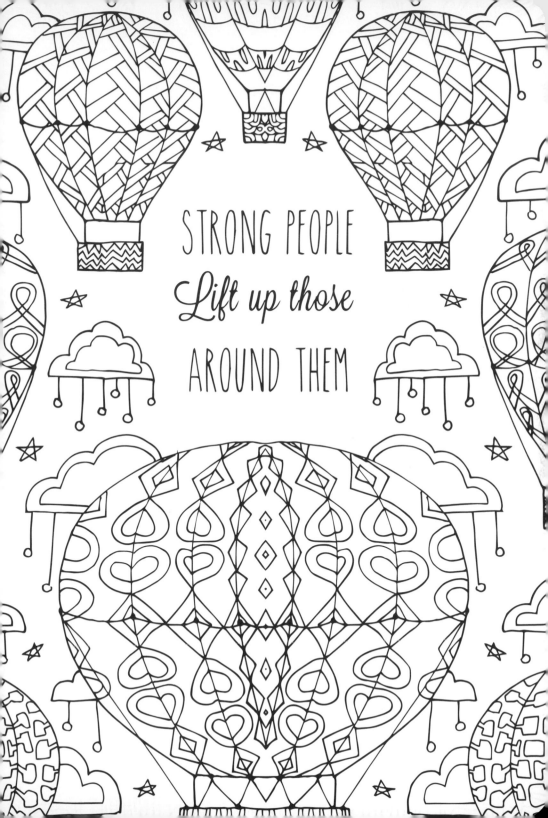

STRONG PEOPLE
Lift up those
AROUND THEM

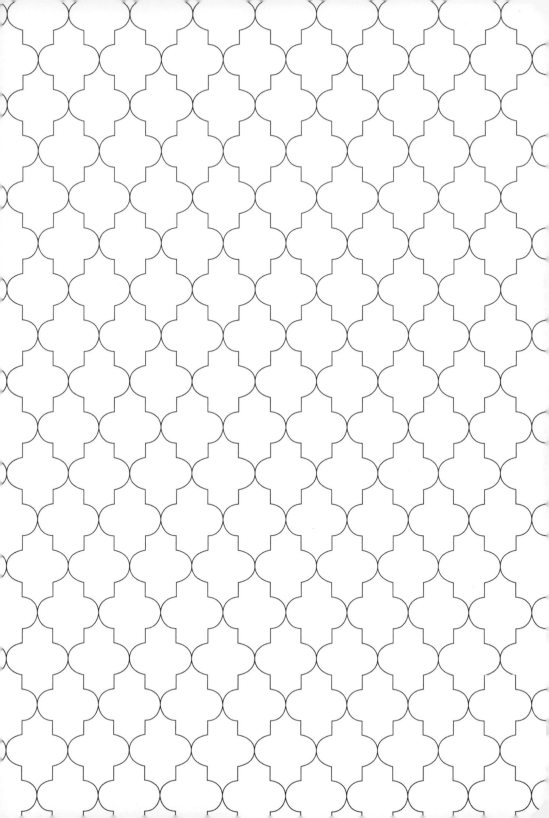

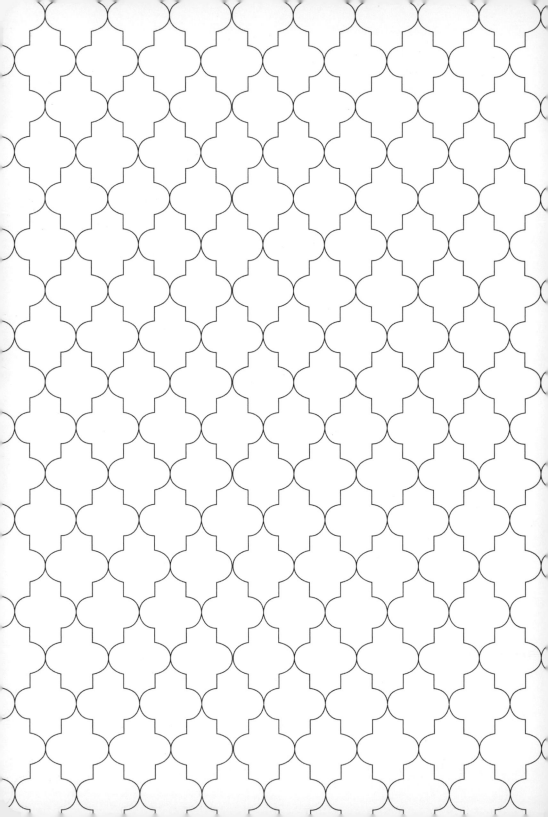